Bonefish Bob
A Tribute

BERNARD F. BLANCHE

Strategic Book Publishing and Rights Co.

Strategic Book Publishing and Rights Co.
12620 FM 1960, Suite A4-507
Houston, TX 77065
www.sbpra.com

ISBN: 978-1-61204-571-9

Book Design: Judy Maenle

Cover artwork: "The Fisherman" (Pastel chalk) by Bernard J.
Blanche, Copper Hill, TN, and photographed by Marilyn Nolt,
Souderton, PA. Back cover photograph: Robert E. Berger,
provided by Wendy Berger Rogers, York Beach, ME.
Cover background: "El Radobe Key Bonefish" by Adam
DeBruin, Key Largo, FL.

Dedication

*This work is dedicated to the family, friends, and fishermen
who have known this man and shared in the wonder
of his life and his stories. I extend my special gratitude to
Suzanne Moffitt for her editorial assistance on this work
and my first novel,* Iracema's Footprint.

Contributors to the Oral Storytelling Tradition

Arthur Berger, York, Maine

James Berger, Dania Beach, Florida

Robert Berger II, York, Maine

Stephen F. Blanche, Key Largo, Florida

Robert Brien, Bristol, Virginia

William Coite, York, Maine

Patrick Cutrone, Norwalk, Connecticut

Kirk Gammill, Missoula, Montana

D. L. Goddard, Easton, Maryland

Dwayne Jellison, York, Maine

Richard McCleod, PGA retired, York Golf and Tennis Club

Richard Mitchell, Islamorada, Florida

William H. L. Mitchell, Portsmouth, New Hampshire

Dr. H. C. Palmer, Lenexa, Kansas

Wendy (nee: Berger) Rogers, York, Maine

David Sowerby, York, Maine

Jan Wood, Ennis, Montana

Judy (nee: Berger) Woods, York, Maine

Table of Contents

Prologue

In the early spring of 2004 when I arrived in Islamorada, Florida, with my son Stephen, Bonefish Bob's shop was closed for lunch. Stephen insisted I meet Bob and said he knew exactly where to find him. South on Route 1 and on the eastern side of the road was Steve's Time Out Bar-B-Q. It was a bright sunny day, the kind that makes you blind when you enter a building. After our eyes adjusted, we found Bob Berger seated at his regular table with his back to the front wall of the restaurant. There were three casually dressed men seated with him. Stephen, Bob, and I chatted briefly, and we left after a short visit. One of the men, as I was later to learn, was D. L. Goddard, an eventual contributor to this tale. It was awkward being an interloper, but the voyage had begun for me.

The stories about Bonefish Bob began accumulating from Stephen, his friends, and others. I was busy finishing the work on my novel, *Iracema's Footprint*, and merely stored these tidbits away. I contacted Stephen finally and asked him to approach Bob with a request of mine. I wanted Bob's consent to tell his story. Just before the end of 2004, Stephen spoke with Bob and I was given permission to write Bob's story. It went on the backburner until I closed the tedious work on my novel.

I began in earnest in the summer of 2006 to collect, research, and organize the details of Bob Berger's amazing life. In York, Maine, I spent a summer's day with Dave Sowerby and William H. L. "Ledge" Mitchell. During our round of golf at York Country Club and a fly fishing trip for stripers, more stories of Robert Berger were shared and recorded.

This is not a biography simply because much of the data gathered, embellished, and retold to me is sometimes impossible to substantiate. Many of the details are accurate, some are exaggerations, some are myths, and some are straight out tall tales. I have attempted to give credit to each contributor for his or her oral story. I have manipulated the timing of some events to facilitate the flow of the work. Some of the scenes are representative of how his friends or even Bob himself may have wanted them to occur, but they never happened—they are dreamscapes of his time alone or the times of unfulfilled plans originally made with the people in his life. There are miracles here, mysteries to fathom, and meanings to learn from this most impressive figure and his astonishing voyage through life.

Chapter One

"As Fragile as Eggs"

In part told to Arthur Berger and
Stephen F. Blanche by Robert E. Berger

M ortars rained in from all flanks, and howling explosions in the cold night air pinned down the GIs on the crest of a little knoll. Sharp flashes of light screamed and ended with a terrifying thump. Some soldiers froze, paralyzed by the fierce war-cry of each burst. Others tried to find the courage to accept whatever fate was to come. After each explosion, a few scurried about dutifully, allowing orders and obedience to replace the nightmare that might suffocate them. Still, there were those who painted the chaos with a fragment of memory. PFC Robert E. Berger from York, Maine, found himself wishing for the smell of salt air. He was pinned, like a striped bass beneath the cold Atlantic awaiting the tease of a fly. The invisible line of the round's trajectory cast the fly to the sea. Bob felt no urge, like the dormant bass, to take the bait. A picture of pond fishermen cut into the image. Their firecracker explosives pounded the secluded schools of pumpkinseeds and small mouth bass. They netted their unconscious prey—he recoiled from his daydream.

His unit was under heavy assault from North Korean infantry. In 1953, this was his Orient, but certainly not the one of mystery and fantasy. Within shallow, quickly excavated foxholes, the Americans labored to return rifle fire to forestall a charge from the enemy lines. Gravity held them to their positions like eggs in a wind-battered nest. Knife points of shrapnel screeched passed his position, and his companions feared each successive detonation. The men to his right seemed to be the primary focus of the fusillade from the enemy's lines. Muffled cries and calls for medics rang out.

Firing his rifle into the area of a flashpoint where a mortar left its hollow tube, Bob sought to stop the bombardment. He did not think about killing, but rather he sensed the shots would flip the switch to the "off" position. The compound would be left in peace.

Dennis "Stony" Van Hook was nearest to him on the ground, facing the attack. He and Bob had been friends since day one of camp. They had a mutual love and respect for the outdoors. Bob's sea-blue eyes glistened above the wry smile that he slid in the direction of Van Hook. His companion's serious countenance did nothing in return, but he also fired into the artillery position. This lanky Midwesterner had come to boot camp from Indiana. His farming heritage left him painted by earth, sun, and wind. Bob had sensed a bond with the stranger. Despite sharing little in common with him, the sea-mask, which had tanned and roughened Bob's face, made them a pair of brothers of the out-of-doors. The stocky, efficient frame that Bob carried through the drills was athletic and quick, but his motions were always tempered by his study of the moment. Dennis soon became "Stony" to Bob; his rough and somewhat rigid mannerism endeared Bob to his depth and honesty.

In his foxhole, Bob was keenly aware of the softness of the human sounds. He sensed the decibel pitch of each shell's whine as it mixed with the human voices of his boot camp comrades. The metallic and monstrous noise humbled their pleas for aide. His friends' entreaties dare not betray their pain and fear to the enemy, and so they whispered. More and more as he focused on them, he realized that the attack seemed to be waning. As the chaos diminished, his concentration on his unit increased.

A brutal roar of demonic force flung Bob rudely into the air. The microsecond blast of light stole his sight briefly, and the thundering blast robbed him of his hearing. He lit like a crumpled newspaper onto one side. *A concussion* he thought. Instinct etched into his dulled consciousness. He made a quick self-evaluation, *No pain, dead silence outside, ringing inside.*

2

Bob moved and wriggled his shaken body onto his belly. He peered about trying to focus on his surroundings, and it took a few seconds before anything took shape. His sight recovered quickly, but he was aware of stark silence. After he determined his condition internally, he began an outward search.

To his left and pressed against a large boulder like the egg of an insect on the water's edge was a limp figure. The uniform was trim above his waist, but it was tattered, disheveled, and bloodied about his legs. Van Hook did not call out, but Bob still searched his friend's face for words. There were none. In a vacuum, Bob crawled on unfeeling elbows to the side of his wounded companion.

No one came to his cries: "Medic! Medic!" He could not hear his own voice. He never looked to the others to see if they were coming. He assessed Stony's critical condition, stood recklessly, grabbed Van Hook under his shoulders, and lifted him. Curiously, he did not sense the wounded man's weight. Scurrying in retreat, he now scanned the turmoil, seeking any assistance for his injured friend.

Beyond the battle and over the crest of the hillock were triage areas already occupied by the wounded and their medics. No one was free to take Van Hook's limp form from Bob. He trudged farther back from the battle line and down the hill. Bob hoped to locate someone to take his charge from him, for he sensed a duty to return to his position. *There's no round hole for a round peg!* he mused. When he turned and looked back, no recognition came from those he had just passed. The momentary halt brought the recognition of an odor, warm and repugnant. Stony and the blood, sweat, fear, and chemical smoke were part of his every breath.

Refocusing on his mission, he spotted a lieutenant's jeep sitting roadside, a distance from his position. Two soldiers rushed into his line of sight from the road. Reinforcements were arriving in droves along the dirt road. Their faces addressed Bob and spoke excitable words at him, but he heard none of them. His blank face and wide, gem-faceted eyes answered them sufficiently, and the soldiers let him pass quickly. A surreal image of

3

a lobster sheltering eggs on her abdomen flitted across his mind's eye. He was not thinking; he was laboring, and the challenge to secure a safe haven for his wounded friend was agonizing.

PFC Berger plodded downhill with the boot camp numbness of a forced march and full pack. At the jeep, he saw the ignition key in the lock, and he quickly laid his wounded friend carefully in the back compartment of the jeep. He took the driver's seat without a thought and shouted to no one, "Damn it! Seat's back too far!" He made a quick adjustment, turned the key and swung the vehicle around. He sped south toward a MASH unit he had seen on his way to the front.

Bob Berger began to think again, to evaluate, to plan. Van Hook's wounds were severe. Blood was trickling from lesser injuries on his thighs, arms and torso. Bob could not remember if Stony still had his boots on or not. The jeep slammed to a bucking halt. Jumping onto the roadbed, he had already pulled his belt from the loops around his waist. When he tied his belt and then Van Hook's around each leg, he realized that he never suspected that Stony might already have died. Amid the blur of chaos, the thought had never entered his mind. Behind the wheel again, he reached back and tried to feel his patient's throat; but, when his initial attempt proved fruitless, he decided that he did not want to know. Five minutes was all he needed to reach the MASH unit. He tried to calculate the time since the blast. Had it been five or six minutes or was it a half an hour? "There's time, Stony!" mumbled Bob to his passenger.

Dust and dirt coiled about the rear of the fleeing jeep. For the first time, Bob was aware of thirst, for the dirt had crept into his mouth and nostrils. He spat out the left door opening. It was an angry act, but one that left him energized. He remembered a pep talk from a high school coach which precipitated waves of emotions. Within him, there arose doubt, confusion, fear, great sadness, concern, and fatigue. The neap tide of feelings drew tears into Bob's eyes. He fought them back, pressed them with the sleeves of his uniform, and tried to keep his vision clear. He saw the MASH unit up ahead at the next bend.

Two orderlies ignored Bob and immediately took positions at the rear of the jeep as it bucked to a halt. Bob neglected the clutch momentarily until it reminded him of itself with a bounding tantrum, threatening to stall. The servicemen were engaged in conversation with each other and may have even spoken to Bob directly, but he still could hear nothing. The wounded soldier was stretchered and carried from Bob before he could offer any explanation. Bewildered, he stood alone beside the jeep. Euphoria was present, brought about with the completion of a difficult and stressful task; but, deep within him, the pleasant satisfaction wrestled with sadness and longing. He had every intention of waiting to speak to doctors or nurses about his friend Stony, but there he stood like a useless fixture in the MASH triage area. More vehicles arrived, and Bob floated like a cork in a sea of the injured and wounded, medics, and staff.

"Who left that jeep here?" ordered an officer exiting the front of the hospital tent.

Bob attempted to understand the words, for the man was pointing at the vehicle which he had commandeered at the front. PFC Berger made a feeble effort to raise his hand as if petitioning the sergeant to repeat his question but opted to step forward, stand at attention and shout out, "Sir, I can't hear what you said, but I guess you want to know something about the jeep I brought."

It was obvious that Bob was having trouble hearing for the sergeant noted the volume of his first comment. Motioning Bob to set himself at ease, the officer pulled him closer with a wave of his upturned right hand. "You've been at the front?" he yelled, trying to force hearing with a louder pitch.

Bob shrugged his shoulders and cupped his right hand around his ear. The message was understood, and the officer reached into a left breast pocket and produced a pad and pencil. *Get that jeep back to where you got it!* was scrawled on the white lined paper.

"I wanted to wait with my buddy, Sir. He's hurt, Sir" informed Bob in an artificially loud delivery.

A lapse of concentration caused the officer to attempt a further conversation. "I'm no medical officer, Son, but you need to return that vehicle. So get it out of here," he advised. There was a hint of unheard compassion in his voice, and Bob tried to read his face. "What unit are you with? I'll try to get an update to the lines for you about your friend." Then he remembered that the soldier before him could not hear. There was no indication that the officer felt Bob might also need medical attention. He simply wrote *Your Unit?* and *His Name?*

"We're with the 302nd battalion, Sir, and he's Private Dennis Van Hook," sounded Bob.

Writing down that piece of information, the officer drew his eyes from the paper to Bob who read concern and fatigue on the officer's face. Out of all decorum, Bob approached him and, with delicate humanity, embraced the officer. Military training finally took him from the man, and he stepped away and paused. A smile from the officer confirmed his understanding, and he dismissed Bob. With Private Berger's about-face, the sergeant disappeared into the confines of the tent.

Bob prodded the jeep into a sputtering start. He was soon headed back to the front, passing some more reinforcements as they continued in a queue along the road.

Word never came to the front. Bob and the U. S. Eighth Army were immersed in the skirmishes of the Korean Conflict, and other concerns were put aside. A gnawing anxiety kept Bob from a decisive attempt to learn about Stony's fate. Somehow he had already accepted the death of his boot camp friend, and he did not want to relive the agony of mourning. His lack of courage pained him; but not as much, he figured, as knowing for certain that Private Van Hook had indeed died, or that he carried a dead man down that hill in North Korea.

The events of his eastern tour of duty blurred and smudged in definition after the armistice was signed on July 27, 1953. Bob made a deliberate choice to bury those facets of his experiences which left him burdened and feeling less the man. Some of the combat-trained actions he took and the military orders that he followed during the conflict were contrary to his gentleness and humanity. He vowed to cherish and enjoy the companionship of others. Bob Berger carried the army home to York, Maine, like a steamer chest or foot locker, but he deliberately misplaced the key.

Chapter Two

"Fish in the Stormy Curl"

As told in part by David Sowerby,
Arthur Berger, and William "Ledge" Mitchell

York is a tranquil, seaside town on the southern tip of Maine. Brightly colored boats sit in its safe harbor along the York River. Slips, filled with commercial fishing boats, personal craft of all types, and local striper charter boats dot the banks. A heavy rush of dark, brackish water pushes south and eastward along its journey toward the sea. The York swirls in bountiful eddies into bays and cuts. Big fish settle into these resting areas awaiting bait fish, and the guides seek them out with self-tied flies and stout nine to twelve weight fly rods. The York Golf and Tennis Club, on the river's eastern shore, leaves its manicured mark on the scene.

Robert Edward Berger was born in Jamestown, North Dakota, on August 1, 1934, but the family moved to York. He grew into his teens feasting on an abundance of experiences which Maine had to offer. He consumed the out-of-doors, learning the secrets of the coast. It was no surprise to the locals that fishing and the automotive business lured him back to Maine after the war. There he sought the comfort, security, and orderliness of life which he had cherished as a youngster. His brother, Arthur, started him in the car business, and they would trade tools, clients, and knowledge freely. His mother, Luella, eventually owned a garage that Bob took over to repair Saabs and Volvos.

The fresh, salt air never ceased to refresh Bob with every breath. Despite his short stature, Bob carried a manly presence on his rounded frame. His friends readily welcomed his arrival at the docks and looked forward to sharing stories of the fishing when the day was done. He continued to savor the experiences and to mature with them. "Settling in" meant starting a family and taking on the responsibilities of being a contributing member to the community.

The war left him a different person, a new version of the lad who trekked off to the other side of the world. The motives that drove his adventure to the Orient were now lost completely or were deliberately hidden within his private and secured foot locker. Outwardly, a jovial, fun-loving storyteller and sometimes prankster immerged and surfaced. The tomato fight at his garage with Harold Sussman was told by the golf pro, Dick McCleod, many times. This persona provided the safety of a shelter for Bob. People rarely became too serious around him. They knew him to sidestep deep academic questions about life, the past, or people's motives. His joy of life and his energy supplanted anyone's urge to delve into more cerebral matters. However, he took a liking to cribbage and chess—like a man smoking a pipe, he looked like the *Thinker*. To an extent, that was to become a part of his intrigue, and he wore it well.

Selling tires, domestic and foreign cars, and even bicycles kept him from the water more than he liked. He taught himself to discern the quality of antique fly rods and reels. Any spare time he had, he would hustle to dockside and steal moments of rest and relaxation with a fly or spinning rod in his hands.

One particular rough day, motivated by his own private reasons, he took his "Eagle," a North American open deck model, out into the ocean to fish the surf line. A storm had kicked up quite a fuss and left the day dark and foreboding. Few boats left the harbor that day. Wind driven gusts buffeted even the larger boats that attempted to leave the mouth of the river. On this chilly autumn day, Bob sought the challenge.

Dave Sowerby and Bill "Ledge" Mitchell, two friends of his from York, heard later in the day that Bob was out striper fishing. Dave was the taller of the friends; and he, like his companion, Ledge, was athletic and fearless in his youth. "Bob can't possibly have gone out?" bemused Dave.

Ledge cocked his head toward the question and agreed, "I doubt it!" They denied as rumor the information that they received earlier until they noticed the empty space at the Eagle's slip. Bob and his boat were out. It was approaching meal time, and they suspected that he would have returned by now. "You think he might be in trouble out there?" wondered Ledge with a bit more Mainer dialect spurred by his concern.

"Who knows?" contributed Dave, and then he added in a quick, knee-jerk reaction, "We could try to get out and check on him."

Ledge had considerable experience at the helm since his father had put him on boats of all sizes since he was a boy. "Let's give it a try. I'll bet he's off the breakers up by Nubble Point." They knew that Bob liked to fish south of Nubble Lighthouse, just off the schoolhouse which sat on the knoll above the cliff.

The run through the breakers at the mouth of the river was crisp and rapid, fed by the outrushing of tidal water. "It won't be easy getting back in," advised Dave. He pictured Bob navigating his smaller Eagle. "We should try to pilot Bob into the harbor," suggested the taller man.

"You know he won't let us do that," figured Ledge. He maneuvered the craft north toward the lighthouse along the coast but quite a distance from the breaking surf. They focused their sight on the lighthouse and the crashing waves that pounded its foundation.

The lighthouse rose Phoenix-like astride an adjacent flat roofed building. Both were trimmed in fire engine red paint. The light pulsed in rhythmic flashes as the beacon swung on its axis. The keeper's house sat ocean side and was a well-kept, two story home accented by a bright red peaked roof. It was wrapped with a skirt of gray paint around the visible foundation. Two smaller out-buildings dotted the craggy terrain on the property.

After twenty minutes, they determined that Bob and the Eagle were not at the Nubble Lighthouse. Ledge spun the boat southward and tighter to the huge rolling surf. Each successive swell of the ocean stretched its black back upward like a rousing cat before it tore itself into angry, white thunder. Neither man thought about making a few cast for any stripers that might be chasing bait in the tumult. The whole world was charcoal: sky, beach, cliffs, and sea. Shades of slate were broken by the billows of white thrashing foam that chased after the breaking waves. The shards of whiteness fought to conceal any boat in the sea before them. In a minute, Ledge throttled up and headed farther south.

"Wait Ledge, I see something," shouted Dave. His height gave him a crow's nest advantage over his shorter companion. He picked up the flat line of a steadier white smear to the west just off the breaker line. Slowing, Ledge aimed the bow into the sight line of Dave's pointed request, "Over at two o'clock . . . there!" shot Dave.

With its bow anchored to the north, the Eagle was rolling in dance with eastward arriving waves. "There's a lot of anchor line out," reported Ledge with concern etched into the words.

"That's why it hasn't capsized yet," shouted Dave with some fear in his pitch. "I don't see anyone in the boat," he muttered. Dave moved forward of the console to get a better perspective.

"There's something sticking up from the center of the boat," reported Ledge. "But I'm positive that there's no one on board. I'm pretty sure it's Bob's boat, though," continued Ledge with a voice spiced with anxious concern.

"Go up alongside," directed Dave who spun into action. He gathered a life vest and some rope. Ledge pulled within shouting distance. Dave bellowed, "Hey, Bob, where are you?"

It was Ledge who answered, "Dave, that's a spin rod sticking up from the deck of the Eagle!"

"Don't you guys come any closer or you'll cut me off my striper," came the firm warning from the bowel of the Eagle. Still no one was visible on board.

Shocked, but seemingly forced to answer, Dave politely petitioned the bodiless voice, "Is that you, Bob?" He could now see the taut line and the deep bend in the rod. Dave did not await an answer from the boat. "You got a good sized one on as far as I can tell from the bend in your rod."

"Sure do," echoed the voice from the deck of the storm tossed boat, ". . . Been fighting it for ten or fifteen minutes." Then with a choppy digression, he added, "Didn't I tell you guys they loved live eels in the surf off of this point." The rod slammed downward onto the gunwale. Bob could be heard enjoying the moment with exclamations abounding: "Wow . . . Hold on . . . Crap . . . Whoa, no, you don't!" Then a piece of calm settled into the dark afternoon, and Bob narrated, "I couldn't stand up . . . thought I'd go overboard if I didn't lie down!" That was his reasoning, and both Dave and Ledge understood it. The boat continued to yaw and pitch, but the line stayed tight.

"You goin' to need any help, Bob?" volunteered Ledge. The two men shrugged their shoulders at each other realizing that Bob had everything under control. Dave and Ledge would have been embarrassed to admit to Bob that they had come out on a rescue mission of sorts.

"No, you guys go on fishing. Don't worry about me," assured Bob.

"Sure, Bob," and then in an aside to his boating companion, "Ledge, Bob thinks we're out here fishing just like him."

"I'm going to let him think that, too, Dave," whispered Ledge almost reverently. He could not, however, resist one last shouted appraisal, "Bob, maybe now you'll consider that offer you got to buy a bigger boat!"

"Nah!" was tossed back to him much like an unwanted piece of fish bait.

The two friends pulled back at a distance, enough to see Bob's head pop up occasionally above the gunwale. His fish swam in quick, darting runs up and down the shore line. Unlike Hemmingway's circling, powerful marlin testing Santiago, this fish courted Bob with sleek, short flashes of light and speed. He was married to the moment. Ledge and Dave watched him kneel as he hauled the large striper into the Eagle. He jumped in joy when the fish was on the deck, but he quickly dropped onto his knees again to gain stability. He devoured ravishingly these lessons in life—the life he was growing into, the one he chose.

The two friends monitored Bob's progress as he trimmed up the boat and pulled up anchor for his return to harbor. With an air of nonchalance, the two friends managed to trail the boat back to York.

At dockside, as if Bob was suddenly aware of their secret motivations, he threw a feverish handshake at Dave and surprised Ledge with an ample embrace. Bob introduced the trophy striper to the pair like a newfound friend.

Ledge and Dave left Bob at his mopping and cleaning chores and headed to Norma's Kitchen. "When did Bob become a hugger?" Ledge bemused of his friend. When no answer surfaced, he added, "I'd love to have seen Bob standing in *that* boat fighting *that* fish." He bellowed the word, "that," each time he used it. "*That* little man would have been doing some fancy stepping, I bet!" exclaimed Ledge.

Bob Berger had returned home without much fanfare and dropped the Korean memories deep into his psyche like a heavy anchor in still water. He rarely spoke of the events in Asia, for the images of his army career were a source of torment, like childhood nightmares and questions he fitfully left unanswered.

In harbor at York that evening, however, the boy was present in the man, and everyone in Norma's Kitchen shared in the revelry of Bob's day of fishing in the storm. Ledge and Dave felt free to add their contributions to the tale, and the site of the battle was touted as "Berger's Bend, just a quarter mile south of Nubble light." Bob Berger was on firm ground and at peace. The evening ended with a confession from Bob. "You know, Ledge, I think I do want to speak to that guy about a bigger boat?"

Chapter Three

"...It's the Size of the Fight in the Fish"

As told in part by David Sowerby, Arthur Berger, and William Mitchell

---

Besides Dave and Ledge, quite a few other fishermen drifted into the proximity of Bob and were drawn to his magnetic grip. The commercial charter guides began to stalk the Eagle when it went out of the harbor. Bob built a dependable reputation scouting out schools of sport fish. The charter captains usually moored just a short distance off the Eagle to guarantee their clients a productive catch. Bill Coite also showed up on occasion to get an earful of the newest sagas coming out of the harbor. Then Dwayne Jellison became entwined in the aura of fishing, the sea, and the presence of Bob Berger. The camaraderie of Norma's Kitchen or Rick's Cafe was warm and nurturing in the winter months and refreshing, cool, and restful in the summer. The spring and fall took care of themselves.

Art, the senior member of the Berger clan, related the frustration of one recent striped bass trip in the Atlantic to the salts assembled at the cafe. The brothers tried every fly, plug, and live bait they brought on board that day but still had not coaxed even the slightest strike from the waters around Nubble Lighthouse.

"So Bob and me, we figured on a short day out there," resolved Art to the attentive tars. Bob was present, but held to a stoic posture, allowing his older sibling to manipulate the tale anyway he pleased. "Bob got to pacing up and down the deck mumbling to himself," pictured Art. "Finally, I asked him what he was spouting off about. He stops walking and looks at me with a wrinkled up puss and says that we got to start thinking like the fish. Well, I told him that I thought we had been doing that all morning long. But he shakes his head and says that we still hadn't figured them out. 'Wouldn't they be biting if we did?' he asks me. Then he began to look around again and said, 'The bass have seen everything we have, but nothing they like. We need something different.' He had taken off his old plaid flannel shirt and thrown it onto the bench near the consul. It was red, black, and had some green thread in it. Before I can say or do anything, Bob's torn a piece right off the bottom of that shirt. Next thing I know, he's rigging it onto one of his flies. He spits out the whole wad of tobacco that he was chewing and says, 'Have to try something or go home empty handed!' I'm telling you guys I could not believe my eyes. That first cast and, wham, he gets this tremendous strike. That striper weighed fifteen pounds at least. Now I figure I have to have my piece of that flannel shirt, and I hook up immediately. Fellows, we landed nineteen rockfish in one hour, and those bits of plaid held up all morning." When Art finished, he was breathless before an audience full of smiles and laughter. Bob leaned over and planted a one armed hug on his older brother.

Robert E. Berger married Lois and started a family. The business became Robert Berger and Sons even before the boys grew into it. The brood grew and cookouts and barbecues fed the memories of the children. The eldest girl, Judy, was quick to find her father in a crowd. Her younger sister, Wendy, grew into age dancing and flitting about Bob's feet. The elder son, James, avoided the tag of "Junior" when Bob chose not to name him after himself. Jim inherited more of the wanderlust of his father than did the rest of the offspring. He eventually settled in Dania Beach, Florida. The younger son was Robert II, who preferred the diminutive moniker of "Robbie". He kept, however, the "II" attached formally after his adult signature. He became the family representative in York when Bob finally moved south. Robbie ran his businesses and kept in touch with Mom, Uncle Art, and the girls.

Occasionally, the children and the wives joined the group at the local eateries. The youngsters usually scattered about the restaurant when they arrived. They were often oblivious to the central position that Bob held in the gathering of men who were there well before any of the families arrived. It was a special event for the Bergers to have dinner out, and they frequently gravitated to Norma's for their celebrations. At Norma's Kitchen, the tables were rectangular, paper covered tables. They were heavy and hatch-sized, constructed of wooden planking from aged, abandoned ships that no longer had any use for their skeletal timbers. The locals, expectant of meals and stories, ales and stronger liquors, rubbed them smooth with eager elbows and hands that stretched and slid across their surfaces.

On one October Saturday afternoon in the mid 1960's, following a productive morning of striper fishing, the usual band of friends was seated around one of the window tables. Some looked out into the autumn harbor scene with a sense of quiet fatigue; others sipped beer and offered mundane conversation. Contentment marked the mood of the men, and no one seemed willing to energize the conversation with any worthwhile recounting of the day's events. Bill and Dwayne tasted their drinks and let their vision drift around the room. Ledge and Dave had slid back in their chairs and mutually stretched their legs. Bob straddled his captain's chair, placing his feet on either side of the front legs. There was no desire to ruin the tranquility with trivial banter. The group, however, seemed poised for some auspicious event, some worthwhile occurrence, to feed and lure them from their complacency.

Eventually, the conversation involved Bob's options to buy a Chris Craft that Ledge's father used in Florida at Ocean Reef. Ledge tempted him with it, and it became one of the catalysts that would eventually lure him south to Florida.

A sharp shaft of sunlight shot into the dining room accompanied by a gust of crisp salt air. A backlit figure remained at the doorway, momentarily surrounded by the autumn day that had followed him into Norma's Kitchen. When he spotted the locals, he directed his purposeful steps toward them at their window perch. Only one arm swung in cadence to his walk, for the other remained akimbo at his waist. Matt Corey had on his old jeans and still wore a fishing vest overtop of his well-worn, light-weight, long sleeved shirt. The local fishermen were now protecting themselves from the sun's rays with clothing or thirty plus sun block. Matt chose the clothing over the creams.

After a few strides, Dwayne noticed the baggage that Matt wielded with his right arm. "Well, whatcha got here?" he cast at Matt.

Pleased that someone had noticed his package, Matt proudly announced, "Oh, just a little something!" The answer was delivered with flair, and his self-indulgence oozed from his personal elaboration. "Now this *here* is a striper!" With his entrance completed, he slapped the ten pound fish onto the paper tablecloth. He grinned with his head tossed back and his chest pumped upward.

"That sure is a nice fish," agreed Ledge with a nod of his head but with muted excitement.

"Yep, that could be somebody's personal best, I'll bet," ventured Dave with some encouragement.

Bill Coite wanted a little more information. "What did ya get him on?" he asked with some honest concern.

"He took one of my own green deceivers . . . smacked the living daylights out of it!" Matt's excitement pulled the breath from his body. He took a big refreshing gulp of air.

Dwayne was the first to realize that the fly was still in the striper's mouth. He reached over to tug at it and surmised, "That the fly there, Matt?"

"Sure is," he beamed. "I'm going to tie a few more of them. That's for sure!" By now Matt was doing a little jig and began leaning toward the location of the restrooms. "Be right back!" he stammered, already on his way to the bathroom.

Bob stood and pulled back his chair just enough to permit his passage from the table. Maneuvering to leave, Bob pushed his chair under the top of the table.

Ledge halted him with an outstretched left arm. "You have to keep Matt company, Bob?" was his effort at a joke. Ledge's

17

left arm dropped from its resting point when Bob reached forward and picked up the fish. Ledge thought Bob was trying to feel the weight and added, "What do you think it weighs, Bob?"

Bob looked him straight in the eye and, with a glint of mischief in his own, rocked his head left and right and shrugged in response to Ledge. He began to creep away from the table with the fish in tow. Still no words came from Bob.

"Where ya going with that?" flung Dave into Bob's retreating frame. The thief charged the front door, scurrying off with Matt's pride and joy. Still there was no comment from Bob.

"He's up to something," bemused Ledge to his companions with a statement of the obvious, but no one made the least effort to detain or even stop him. Bob and the fish were gone. "I hope Matt doesn't get outta joint," he mumbled.

Everyone was quietly reflective when they saw Matt returning to the table. Like a table of kindergarten students who knows one of their tablemates has done something amiss, they hung heads, drummed fingers, twitched, and looked askance as Matt approached. The fish was not immediately missed, for Matt had no reason to suspect that it would have left the table.

With a tilt of the head that spoke of disbelief, he queried, "Hey! Where's my striper?" Silence, shrugs, and eyes veering from contact with him served as answers. "Come on, guys! What's going on?" he begged in his second attempt at information.

Dave never could stand to have someone befuddled around him. It did not seem fair that everyone knew something that the victim did not. Holding off as long as he could, Dave finally confessed, "Bob got up, picked it up, and walked out the front door with it." His duty done, he was not about to say anything more.

A swoosh of air moving, a shaft of autumn light exploding, and a perception of something moving replaced any further conversation. All heads turned to the front entrance. A spark-plug of a figure was heading toward the group lugging a sack-like burden draped over his right shoulder. The myriad of activity, backlit by sunlight cascading upon them, kept at bay the identity of the intruder. He was upon them in seconds.

"Bob!" rang out from several sources. An avalanche of motion, a heavy thud, and a blur of silver and black crashed onto the table. All eyes examined the bundle.

With the timing of a stage comedian, Bob hesitated for a two-count and dropped the punch line, "Now, *that's* a striper!" The "that's" erupted like a whip crack behind a wry smile. On the flat surface before them lay an immense fifty inch or better striped bass. Curiously, it held within its maw another striper, smaller and narrower in girth. Protruding from the monster's jaws was the tail end of the lesser fish. A foot of tail section was visible jutting from the mouth of Bob's fish.

With an air of humble certainty, Matt reached over, pried open the mouth, and slowly withdrew the second "rockfish" from the giant's maw. When the green deceiver could be seen, all was confirmed as to the whereabouts of Matt's specimen. Bob snuggled over to his victim and reached his right arm over Matt's shoulder. He pulled the friend to him in a bear hug, and they shook in unison with Bob's repeated, staccato vice grips.

Laughter rang loudly at Norma's Kitchen that evening and even Matt was pleased to be a part of the lore. Pictures were taken before the fish were dispatched to their final rests, but it was the turn of events, not the photos, that would linger in memory.

Chapter Four

"Hungry Fish Will Strike Twice"

As told in part by William Coite

The snow fell without an accompanying wind. The light, dry crystals settled in deep mounds of icy white. It was a perfect snowmobile snowfall. Bob Fox and Dave Sowerby busied themselves with preparations to head north and run the snowmobiles up at Eustis, Maine. "Fox" as they called him at times, appeared the "middle man" of the trio. His stature placed him between the lanky Dave and the five foot eight Bob. Dressed in their insolated winter garb, the three men could still be recognized by friends because of their various heights. Bob had some unknown chores to run before he joined the two outside Rick's Cafe. Earlier, Fox and Sowerby set their recreational vehicles onto a tandem trailer. Bob pulled up behind Fox's truck in the parking lot. It was late morning, but the truck grill glistened with headlight spray. The heavy fall of snow absorbed most of the illumination provided by the truck and added a muffled solitude to all the sounds of the morning. Bob jumped from his truck and jogged to the driver's side of the companion vehicle.

"Hey, Fox! Roll down your window!" bellowed Bob.

Bob Fox's triangular face eased into view as the window rolled down. His deep set eyes and heavy brows etched his appearance clearly, despite the low lighting in the cab. "We're ready to go," informed Fox, nodding toward Dave.

"You all finished with your chores?" quizzed Dave from the other side with a chuckle of boyishness.

"No!" stammered Bob as if he had been caught copying homework. "I haven't picked up anything for dinner, and I might need some gas," he confessed.

"Well, we want to get going before it gets too late. With this snow, it'll take us four hours. We can stop on the way," decided Fox with anticipation. "You know I love snowmobiling at night with the lights on." He turned the steering wheel of his truck, and that alone signaled to Berger to get into his truck and follow them north.

Three and a half hours into the trip, Bob was flashing his lights to the forward truck. An intersection could be seen up ahead of the travelers. Despite the darkness of the late afternoon and the falling snow, a neon sign and a traffic light could be detected. The two vehicles plowed passed a road sign which read, "Eustis."

On the right side of the intersection and beyond the traffic light, a red and yellow neon advertisement read, "The Kern's Inn." Bob's escorts wheeled into the parking lot which fronted the inn and turned off the ignition. Bob followed suit and, exiting his truck, arrived at his friend's vehicle with his hands jammed into the front pockets of his parka.

"I need to get some gas," puzzled Bob, "but the station is over there on the other side of the highway." With the jerk of his left elbow, he indicated "Tom's Petrol Station" as it blinked with green-lighted trim.

"We decided since you also forgot dinner, we'd stop here for a bite," counseled Fox.

"We still have some miles to go, and there are no more stops along the way," added Dave with an air of fatherliness caused by his familiarity with the area. "You can fill up when we leave here."

Bob accepted his fate as penance for having forgotten to complete his chores. He did not wish to further inconvenience his companions. The Kern's Inn provided passable fare, and the time spent was a needed break from the rigor of driving in a heavy snowstorm. To the three friends, it seemed appropriate to postpone the exhilaration of the nighttime rides on their snowmobiles. It enhanced the excitement – the delay was welcomed.

Outside the restaurant, the riders maneuvered their vehicles across the highway toward Tom's Petrol. It was then that Bob noticed that Tom's Petrol was really "Tom's Petrol and Deli." "Could have made one stop," he grumbled to the icy air in the cabin.

The forward truck drove passed the pumps and allowed Bob to park conveniently beside the end gasoline dispenser. "Attendant Serve Only" read the notice attached to the body of the pump. Bob quizzed himself about the reason a clerk would want to come out on a night like this to dispense gas. He had only a short time to ponder his question, for the door of the deli/gas station swung open and a heavily clothed snowman-sized individual approached his truck.

Fox watched the proceedings from a backward and in-reverse perspective off the reflection of his side view mirror. Dave swung his left arm around and over the bench seat and eavesdropped through the back window. They were both surprised to see Bob exit his vehicle and begin an agitated dance with the attendant. "There's a lot of pointing and waving going on back there," reported Fox.

Dave never took his eyes off the scene behind him. "Bob's throwing some of his 'BS', as usual," assured Dave.

"What's taking the guy so long to pump the gas?" wondered Fox with a bit of growing concern in his tone. They both realized that some negotiation had begun between the attendant and Bob; and, when Bob turned and headed in their direction, they began to formulate an alternative plan.

"My guess, Foxy, is that the guy doesn't have any gas in his pumps!" bemused Dave with a disgruntled pitch to his voice. "I'll bet we're going to have to leave Bob's truck here until we return," groaned Dave as Fox put down his window.

"You guys won't believe this! You will not, freakin', believe this one! No way!" raved Bob as he reached the tandem. "Come on, get out of the truck!" he ordered. Bob reached out, grabbed the handle, and jerked open the front door.

"What the heck for?" stammered Fox as he was now being pulled physically from his own truck. Bob did not think Fox's body would ever clear the cab, but he was already moving into the cab to snag Dave. He began to yank and tug the lengthy

Dave across the bench seat. Dave had his right hand on his doorknob in an abortive effort to exit from his own side of the truck. Bob did not give him that choice. With both men afoot on the ground, Bob silenced their ranting with two upraised arms. His open palms petitioned calm from them and held them at bay long enough for Bob to grin and bleat, "How about me taking you both into the deli for a nice dinner?"

The two men stood incredulous. They exchanged doubtful and confused glances before Dave was able to utter, "Bob, I don't know if you remember or not, but we just ate dinner . . . over *there!*" He pointed weakly in the direction of The Kern's Inn. This met with a knowledgeable nod from Fox who added a forced, but wry, grin as his agreement.

Bob took a breath to organize his thoughts and explained, "Tom, the owner of the gas station and deli here, informed me that I can only get gas if I, ah . . . we, have, ah, dinner at his establishment." He delivered the sentence as if it almost made complete sense to him and to his friends. It did not.

"You've got to be kidding, Bob!" challenged Fox with some annoyance and without any humor. He turned to Dave in a gesture which pleaded for assistance from him in his hour of need. Dave shrugged his shoulders, bit his lip, and stood shuffling from side to side.

"I had a reasonable discussion with this Tom, fellow, and I agreed that we'd stop in for a bite," negotiated Bob. He began to turn toward the deli when Fox reached out and touched his retreating arm.

"You're serious, aren't you, Bob?" returned Fox.

"Sure!" Bob retorted, "I don't want to cost you guys anymore inconvenience, time or trouble because I came on this trip unprepared. Besides, it's my treat."

"Fox, if we're getting something free from Bob, ah . . . even if we really don't want it, I think we should take him up on this silly offer," expounded Dave, sounding like a union mediator. It was obvious that Dave wanted to get on the road as quickly as possible. By his reckoning, disputing this contract that Bob made with the belligerent proprietor was going to use up a lot more of their snowmobiling time than having a "quick bite" as Bob put it.

So the threesome ambled with a mixture of emotions through the still falling snow toward the deli's front door. Bob was buoyant and pleased with himself. Fox strode onward like a convicted felon whose late appeal had gone unheeded by the parole board, and the prison warden had mistakenly provided him with two last meals. Dave muttered with an air of disbelief, "Bob's actually going to treat us to a meal!"

The repast was scant, brief, but filled with more warm stories. Tom kept a safe distance, surfacing only to serve the men, remove their used plates and utensils, and hand Bob the check. Fox's eyebrows shot upward when a tip was indeed included by Bob. The proprietor had not yet made any attempt to fill Bob's tank with the promised reward of gasoline. "This guy, Tom, is he going to pump your gas, Bob?" wondered Fox.

"Sure, as soon as we finish our meal," reported Bob. At that very moment, Fox noticed with relief that Tom had slipped from the deli into the snowstorm and headed to Bob's truck. Bob popped from his seat and tracked the deli/gas attendant into the whitened night.

From the deli, the friends watched the mimed puppet conversation between Bob and Tom as the tank filled. Bob reached up and threw a robust bear hug around Tom's chest. The wrestler's grip sealed the deal.

Dave threw an elbow at Fox and summarized, "There's that hugging thing again, Fox!" They were on their way to Eustis for a glorious evening of snowmobiling and with a delicious tale to tell at Rick's Cafe when they returned.

Chapter Five

"Hard Water Smelt"

As told in part by James Berger

The York freezes in the dead of winter. The thick ice mass rises and falls with ten feet of tidal flow, leaving the hard crust to inhale and exhale above the flow and ebb. Clever and opportunistic residents build comfortable wooden shacks that they skate across the surface and anchor to a favorite spot above the channel. Access can be obtained just below the Scotland Bridge.

Bob Berger never permitted the weather to interrupt his ventures into the subtleties of smelt fishing. He constructed a cabin-like shed which he pushed onto the ice each winter. The insulation was thick and the warmth of a small kerosene heater stayed within its confines. The trap door in the floor allowed for holes to be cut into the ten-inch ice. During the season, the smelt ran in and out of the mouth of the York with each tide.

Bob had to wait for Berger and Sons to close for the day before he could afford a trip onto the York. Frequently, this meant that he would set aside evening hours for the fishing. When Jim, his eldest son, was thirteen, he happened to accompany his father on a particularly cold Friday evening.

They packed up their gear, some sandwiches and an empty bucket that they were sure would soon be filled with smelt. Bob tossed Jim the keys to the car. On occasion, he gave the lad a chance to practice driving. The youngster learned to pull forward in the driveway and then to back down the macadam. It was a treat for him to have the ignition keys in hand and warm up the auto before they set out. "Take some of the gear with you, Jim," petitioned Bob as the eager teen rushed to the front door.

"Sure, Dad!" obeyed the son; and then, in a teasing tone, Jim added to his father, "Don't you go and forget our sandwiches!" The father's gestures of a wink and a smile ushered him out the front door.

The drive to the parking lot by Scotland Bridge was dark with an overcast sky and a sliver of moon. Bob was glad he brought a lantern, for the walk to the shanty could be unsettling as the ice moved with the rise and fall of the water below. They timed their arrival on the incoming tide, just right for the run of smelt into the York River. It was nine o'clock when they parked the car, and the temperature was in the teens. "We'll be cozy in the shed, Son," Bob comforted as he shoveled the keys into his pocket. "But I'll bet it's going to be about ten degrees by the time we get back," he predicted.

"That's okay Dad, we can handle that," boasted the boy. Jim was leaner than his younger brother Robbie, but they shared uncanny resemblances to their father. They had a slow rocking motion to their walks and saw everything through sea-blue eyes. Jim assimilated the out of doors before his siblings grew into their own appreciation of nature. He functioned as the test driver for their experiences in the wild with which their father enriched them. Bob's reward was the youth's excitement and anticipation of the evening's fishing. Jim, like all of the children, enjoyed the teasing and practical jokes of his father. Respectfully, Jim and the others had even begun to emulate his antics.

Like pack mules, the twosome cautiously felt a safe passage-way across the ice toward their little one room shack. Any damage to the surface crust from the most recent high tide might be difficult to detect. Bob lit the lantern and followed Jim; the spray of light dusted the lad's steps with a secure pathway. After a few hundred yards, they entered the shanty and busied themselves with the smelt fishing preparations. Bob lifted the trap door, secured it, and twisted the auger into the solid ice over an old, refrozen scar from the last expedition. Not much conversation originated from the pair as the business-like routine of setting up the night's fishing took precedence. Once the tip-ups and bamboo poles were baited and the lines dropped into the black water beneath the shelter, the companions eased into unhurried chatter.

"So how did your week go, Jim?" asked Bob as he nudged Jim and shot an upraised eyebrow at him. He was seated on the same small bench alongside Jim.

The teen reacted with a crisp turn of his head that placed their eyes upon one another. "You aren't going there, Dad?" begged Jim, who understood his father's non-verbal reference to "the girl".

"I thought maybe you had made some progress with that Linda that I heard you mention to Robbie." Bob did not intend to let him off the hook so easily.

"We're just fr . . . ," he started, but a reflexive grab for the bamboo pole in front of him cut his sentence short. "Got the first one, Dad!" cheered Jim as he hauled a sleek, wriggling smelt out of the darkness and onto the floor. The silvery fish was unhooked and scooped into the bucket nearby with his cupped hands "That's a quarter for me!" Jim celebrated.

"I'll get it back when I catch the most and . . . the last one," challenged Bob.

"No way! Not this time!" Jim found joy in the competitive nature of his father, for he reached a stage in his growth that afforded him more and more opportunities to make any contest a fairer match. He had to concede cribbage to his father, but with physical tests he was making headway.

"We can get a good bucketful by the time the tide runs out if they start hitting this early," addressed Bob to his son, aware that the "girl" issue was finished. Changing tactics, he added, "Classes okay?"

"Sure," responded Jim with an air of nonchalance. "You know I have that science project, and I'm reading *Old Man and the Sea*." He baited the bamboo rod's hook and sent it into the frigid waters.

"Well, if you need my help, let me know," volunteered Bob. The fisherman again switched gears. "Mom would be great out here!" Bob chuckled with a bounce to his shoulders.

"Ha, ha!" retorted Jim with shared amusement. "Come on, Dad. You know that would be a disaster. The cold, the mess, the late hours . . . she'd be way out of her element."

"We'd have to have her walk the plank . . . except we don't have one," remarked Bob.

"At least she wouldn't get seasick out here," laughed Jim as he watched his father pull up his first fish of the night.

The evening waned; the tidal flow arrived, pushing the ice up like a cork. The shanty creaked and spoke its own language, stretching like an old cat rising after rest. The smelt came in schools, some numbers larger than others. Then the outflow began and the process reversed itself. The shed eased itself down with the descending ice, yawning and groaning into repose. The bucket eventually contained a magical volume only known to Bob, and he declared, "Next fish is the last!"

The announcement brought Jim upright from his slumped pose on the bench. His senses rejuvenated by the declaration. Dad was ahead in the count, and Jim wanted to win the last challenge. There was a strike on one of Bob's bamboo poles. Jim slumped, watching the victory slip away.

"Gonna take it easy with this one, Jim. I don't think I have it hooked well," he narrated. Jim knew this was an unusual tactic for his dad to take; for, generally, the smelt were swung into the shack rather than played. "Oops! Dang!" he stammered, "lost it." Bob made a sideways glance toward Jim who sprung upright, resurrected with renewed focus on his lines. A smile seeped onto the man's face as he noted the minute to-and-fro wiggling of the boy's head which accompanied his alerted rocking torso.

"Should've landed that smelt, Dad," countered the teenager, "I've got one, no . . . *two* strikes!" With left and right hands occupied, Jim raised the rods and succeeded in putting two smelt on the floor at the same time. "Wow! I've never got a double like that, Dad!" Grinning broadly, he swung the two wriggling silver knives of light over the bucket and claimed them. "That's the last one, er . . . ones, right?" he coaxed. "I have the first and last." He was quite satisfied with himself but managed to feel some remorse for his father. "You really did well, Dad—you had a great night," he cajoled to Bob.

"I know when I'm beaten," he admitted. "Just for that you carry the smelt back to the car." Bob decided to leave the gear in the locked shed. Jim also picked up the empty lunchbox along with the smelt. Bob shut off the heater and picked up the lantern for the return trek.

The door opened into a frigid, ebony-drenched night. On their first steps, they could sense the slight concave slant of the ice as it stretched toward the bank. "Yeah, it's at least ten degrees out here," mumbled Bob to his son and to himself. It was nearing one in the morning, and the earlier fatigue that Jim felt quickly left him when the northerly breeze hit him. The slope increased as they neared the ice edge. "I'll bet the water's eight or nine feet below the ice by now," calculated Bob.

Bob watched the cautious, but practiced, steps of his son ahead of him. The boy managed the ice walk back to the car and the Scotland Bridge with fearless ease. They had done this before in daylight and once in the night. Bob Berger had a sense of pride in his children and their willingness to take on new experiences and learn from them. He appreciated the respect that each had for the natural world and the joys it gave to them. He maneuvered the arc of lantern light forward and into the path of his son's steps.

Jim slid his feet out in front of himself, skating over the slick surface. He enjoyed the freedom the gliding gave him. Behind him, Bob trod casually forward with a slight waddle. Suddenly, the light was gone. Only the dark northerly wind whistled in the silence. Jim wheeled about, searching for any illumination. Darkness and quiet struck him in the face.

"Dad! Dad!" he called to an answerless evening. "Dad, where are you?" he bellowed with growing urgency; his echo, weakened in its return, distracted the youth. He padded with the toes of his boots, trying to find anything in the darkness. As his eyes adjusted to the soot-painted air, he discerned a darker swath in the ice surface. He approached the spot with reckless haste. Jim could pick out other openings along the bank in an easterly direction toward the mouth of the river. Surface ice had dropped into the receding York River on the ebb tide, leaving splotches of terrifying darkness. A hollow swooshing noise oozed from the nearest gap in the ice. "Dad, where are you?" he yelled with terror, panic in every syllable.

"Don't come any nearer, Jim," erupted like crystalline lava from the bowels of the York River. The calmness of the directive from the unseen speaker challenged the turmoil and fear within the boy. But his bewilderment suffocated him. His father was somewhere below the ice and downstream.

Taking a deep breath, Jim dropped onto his knees, leaving the bucket of smelt and the lunchbox to fend for themselves atop the frozen deck. He crawled passed the first break in the ice on his hands and knees. He saw the shard-like fingers of broken ice that lay downstream of him. "Can I reach you, Dad?" came feebly from his lips. Anguish colored his voice into a quavering and rasping whisper.

"Jim, don't you dare get any closer to me!" ordered Bob. The shout arrived muffled by ten inches of York River ice. Jim was sidling along the surface, keeping in contact with his father's voice which seemed to drift ever-so-slightly downriver. The tide inched into neutral, but sometime soon it would start its course back into the river. Looking downward into the next maw, Jim's vision focused on a dark phantom backlit against a white, pale wall of shore ice. He marked his father's head and arms bobbing along the ice face. The figure rose and grasped a layer of ice above him. There was an explosive crack which recoiled with a spray of water and splash of sound. The figure was momentarily gone but bobbed up again and drifted a bit seaward.

"Dad, I saw you! You're down river from me," coached the boy. He shuffled farther east toward the next break. Bob ceased his drift and kicked furiously at the water with his booted feet. He managed to grasp a hold on a second shelf of ice. This ledge lay higher above the water than his last handhold. Horror entered Jim's mind when he again heard the thunderous fracturing of the ice shelf in front and above his father. Darkness consumed Bob.

"No, no!" prayed Jim into the bleak heavens above him. "Don't let this happen, please."

A sputtering of water and a loud gasp of breath below him brought Jim into the fearsome reality of the moment. Bob was again trying to gain a handhold on the bank of ice. Jim watched helplessly as his father mustered his strength and energy to propel his torso high enough to grab a solid grip on the ice. Flailing and grunting, the figure rose from the abysmal depths. A single arm secured a hold and then the second groped upward onto the same thick step of frozen water.

"Hold on, Dad!" encouraged Jim. The lad was torn—it would be cowardly to flee for assistance, and it would be disobedience to climb down to his father against his orders. Jim agonized over the unpardonable sin of sitting like a spectator in the bleachers while his father perished.

"I can't focus on getting out of here if I have to worry about you coming down here, Jim," arose the cool, resolute decision from below. The calm certainty of the voice and the logic of the statement solidified Jim's choice. He waited painfully and watched with prayer and unbearable fear.

A lumbering black figure emerged from the ebony water. Shoulders, chest, waist, hips, and finally the legs climbed dripping from the icy water into the paralyzing cold. Slowly, with care upmost in his mind, Bob inched his way upward. Each handhold was tested before the next foot placement. Jim willed strength into the barrier ice that connected shore to the surface floe. Only when Bob's arms reached the top of the floating surface did the young man have the luxury of a relaxed breath. Before reaching the summit, Bob signaled with his left hand for Jim to remain back. Obedient, Jim wrestled with his sense of duty; he pressed hips and buttocks back onto the heels of his boots and waited. Finally, his father stood, took two awkward and exhausted steps away from the opening and halted transfixed. In the mischievous northerly wind, his clothing froze hard almost instantly. His outstretched arms and rigid legs set an eerie posture. In backdrop against the wintery sky, he posed like a scarecrow, a sentinel guarding the field of lifeless ice.

"Jim, I need your help now," gushed Bob with an exhaling white cloud of voice and mist that pleaded through his fatigue. Subdued by the ordeal, his tone was powerless. "My clothes are solid ice." Bob wobbled momentarily but gained his balance. Jim skated to his side, anxious to embrace his father. That desire, when presented with the statuesque figure before him, soon dissipated. "Just get the keys from my pocket."

"Okay Dad!" The task was difficult, for it involved the removal of gloves and the prying apart of the slit of his pant pocket. Jim sensed an exhilaration fed by duty and action. Once he had the keys in hand, he searched his father's face for direction. "Now what?"

"Grab the lunchbox and bucket and run and get the car started," he directed. "I'll be right behind you."

Jim rushed forward without a thought as to the maneuverability of his father. Ten paces into his quest, he wheeled about to check on the frozen man behind him. There was no humor in the teetering struggle of Bob as he tipped to one side, stepped and yawed to the other leg. When the car was idling on the lot, Jim returned to the frozen river and his conflicted parent.

"Let me help you, Dad," volunteered Jim. The boy crutched the man and facilitated the journey to the car. Bob's face wore the discomfort and exertion of a marathon runner. His eyes were vacant, fully opened, his mouth contorted and wavy without meaning. In reflexive concern, the lad volunteered, "I love you." Simultaneously, he pondered unspoken a dreadful thought.

Arriving at the bank, the pair circumnavigated the frozen riffles and edges and finally stood on firm ground. The only sound was the engine, the warm solace of rescue. Even the headlights oozed with warmth and a consoling light. "Jim, you're going to have to drive," affirmed Bob with a non-negotiable sternness. "Help me into the back seat."

Jim remembered once helping to transport some dining room chairs in the car. The geometry of the shapes fought the symmetry of the door opening. Bob had too many appendages locked at too many angles. The end result left Bob lying on his right side with his right arm under the passenger side seat and the left arm shooting back toward the rear window. The left boot rested on the ledge of the back window. Jim forced the right pant leg to bend sufficiently onto the rear seat so as to allow the door to shut. When he took the driver's seat, he could look at his father over his right shoulder, for Bob's head rested on the rear bench behind the passenger seat.

"Make sure you're in reverse first, Jim," preached Bob from the back seat. The York River lay before them. Bob felt the car limp backward and stop before proceeding in first gear. He was surprised at the smooth movement of the auto as it entered the highway.

"I'm aiming for the middle of the road," fumbled the youth, "'cause there's not any traffic." He glimpsed backward, but met no sea blue eyes in return. Jim's heart drummed with a dull, basal ache. He swallowed a dry space in his mouth, but pressed the gas pedal with the determination of an adult. Bob was unconscious.

In the driveway, the horn blasts brought help and a chaotic mesh of conversation, oaths, directives and pleadings. The clothes had become pliant with the auto's heater, enough to transport Bob Berger into the parlor of his home. Family surrounded him; the confinement caused by the frozen clothing surrendered under the attack of the warmth of his home. Stripped of the icy clothes, showered, and finally in dry night clothes, Bob nestled into bed. Lois and the four children appeared at his bedside. During the duties that focused on Bob's recovery, Jim narrated the events of the evening to the others.

"I hated to lose that lantern," reflected Bob. The comment left the family incredulous.

"You could have drowned, Bob," proposed Lois who found total agreement from the children wrapped about her.

"Dad, I could have lost you," muttered Jim, reflecting on his unspoken fears.

The children appeared shy and tentative about approaching their father in his "sick" bed. Bob Berger seemed out of place there.

"Lois, it's not like we were being careless or anything," defended Bob. "The damn ice just gave way under me." No visible reaction met his factual analysis of the cause of the near disaster. The stress of the early morning accident drained the family emotionally. With a heavy weariness, Jim numbly leaned with a shoulder on the wall of the bedroom. Bob unraveled himself from the cocoon of his bed, approached Jim, and threw his arms around his son. It was a longer embrace than usual, and it ceased only when Bob moved him to arm's length. "Thanks, Son!" he voiced with the utmost sincerity. Then, with an irresistible afterthought, he added, "I guess I owe you a quarter."

Chapter Six

"Soft Water Smelt"

As related in part by Wendy Berger Rogers

Bob was a mixture of hard and soft when it came to raising children. The garage needed painting, and the older daughter, Judy, agreed to the task in exchange for ten dollars in spending money. After a meticulous and artful daubing of paint on the back wall of Berger and Sons, she expected prompt and full payment. Her impetuous departure from the work site left the paint can open on the ground at the back of the building. The next morning, Judy learned that overnight rain had ruined the remaining paint. Her father charged her ten dollars for the loss of the materials. She was crestfallen, but forever careful about completing a task correctly.

Wendy spent a considerable amount of time coaxing a bicycle from her father. The terms of the agreement were simple: if good money is spent, the bike may never be left outside. Agreement was reached between the parties, and Wendy had her new bicycle. For a few days, there was a strict adherence to the terms of the contract. On the fourth evening, Bob found the bike on the front lawn when he returned home after work. Wendy was already in bed. It was a difficult lesson that Bob served her the next morning. Wendy learned that her prized bicycle was now at the Goodwill Store awaiting some needy child. Commitment to one's word became an intrinsic aspect of the Berger children.

At seven years of age, Wendy was intrigued by the possibility that fish could actually be caught more successfully by making silly faces. After all, that was what her father told her. One warm fall Saturday, Wendy watched her father organizing his light fishing gear. She was anxiously fidgeting nearby, following his every step. Since an early run of fall smelt had come up the York River, Bob was taking her fishing.

"I tell you, Wendy, just ask Jim how many smelt he caught with that cross-eyed blowfish face he makes," advised Bob of his littlest daughter. His back was turned to her as he collected the gear from against the side wall of the house. He spoke the words, however, with a teacher's believability. Wendy stepped backward quickly as Bob turned upon her in transit to the car with an armful of bamboo poles, pails, and a lunchbox. "Whoops, almost got you there, Wendy!" he warned.

"I can make some good faces, Daddy," she said as she tagged closely behind her father. "Jim's not as good at it as I am."

"Well, Honey, then you'll probably get more fish than Jim," encouraged Bob, busily loading the car. The rest of the Berger family had other agendas on this particularly calm autumn day. The sun brought warmth into the stillness, and Bob needed to be out-of-doors. Wendy was his likely candidate for an excuse to go fishing. "We are going to catch a mess of smelt for your bucket!" he promised.

The trip to the parking lot at the Scotland Bridge was filled with childish dreams and tales of exaggerated voyages. The windows were down, and their voices were raised. "We might get a hog-tarpon fish, Wendy," egged her father. Her face squinted in disbelief. "They're like silver carp with pig noses." He saw her question mark grimace. "Honest, Wendy, they eat pieces of mackerel, just like we're going to use."

"Could they pull me in?" wondered the child. "They don't have teeth, do they?" she countered. She watched her father eye the road. Wendy nervously toyed with her fingers as they rested in her lap.

"Nah! Hog-tarpon are little bitty things with gums, no teeth at all," instructed Bob. His sideways glance caught her stretching taller in the passenger seat, relaxed with the newest report from Captain Bob.

Father Bob prepared the bait by dicing a frozen mackerel into small cubes for the size 10 smelt hooks. He figured Wendy was good for a two-hour fishing day. The water level was still a few hours from the high tide, so the current was manageable even with the light bamboo rods. With all of the set up done, Bob turned to Wendy. Her elfin face was flushed red and puffed in a grotesque caricature of some unknown gargoyle. "Practicing, huh?" queried Bob as he led her to a suitable fishing spot.

"Yep!" responded the little lady. The comment dismantled her fish face but left it with a bashful hue. "I'm ready, Dad. I've got the pail," she exclaimed already on her way to the water's edge.

"Hold on there, Young Lady! You wait for me." Bob was hustling after her with his bundle of gear bobbing about his burly frame. The pace exaggerated his familiar swagger. When he reached her, his complexion mimicked his daughter's in its pinkish hue.

For a time, disappointment seeped into the pleasant day. No smelt were enticed by Bob's mackerel or Wendy's faces. Bob worked to find the correct combination of depth, bait size and location along the bank. He figured that the fish had not yet reached the bridge during this tide. Wendy ceased her little nervous dance and plopped down in a heap between two bamboo poles. They showed no signs of being of any interest to her. She had her head clasped in both hands, and a frown hung upon her face. Her father approached her and knelt along side of the sulking child. As he settled back on his heels, he calculated that his fishing trip was going to be considerably shorter than he wished.

"Wendy, you're not making any fish faces," began Bob.

"They don't work, Dad," she whispered, as if the secret was an embarrassment. "I even tried Jim's cross-eyed blowfish puss, and it didn't work."

Bob imagined that the trip hung in the balance if a smelt did not soon strike. He sought any delaying tactic that would give him a fighting chance. "Well, Wendy, try another face," he begged.

"My face is tired," she sulked.

"Come on, Hon! You might just need a tune-up on one of those that you already tried," he encouraged.

She looked up into her father's sea blue eyes and sensed an urge to please him. "Let's see!" she said, "how about this one?"

37

Her childish eyes bugged out; she dropped her chin with her mouth remaining shut. Her hands stretched her forehead skin above her brows.

"Wow! That's impressive!" rooted Bob. "That might do it!" He saw Wendy's eyes roll toward the river bank and the rod tips, searching for the tell-tale flick of a strike. The bamboo remained still.

"See! I'm not good at it anymore, Dad," was her evaluation. She gave up the face.

Bob checked his watch and scanned the water level. "Look, you just need to adjust your face maybe," he stalled. "Try to do the cross-eyes with that face."

"No, it won't work, Dad." She succumbed, humbled and dejected.

"Give it one more try for me, Wendy!" urged Bob like a gambler placing his raise on the table.

"Alright," she consented. Her roundish face contorted with bug eyes, a dropped chin, closed mouth, and the brow skin being pushed upward. Still the bamboo remained stoic.

"Now add the cross-eyes," directed Bob.

Obedient to his wishes, Wendy held the positions of her favorite fish face and then added the cross-eyes. A tense, breath-less moment passed as she waited, and Bob peered at the lines dipped into the York River. Wendy never saw the nibble, but her father broke her from her entrenched fish face. "Wendy, your bamboo pole, grab it!" he shouted.

The child immerged nimble and quick from her cross-legged seat on the bank. She was upon the pole as the smelt pulled downward on the mackerel offal. An elated smile greeted the captured fish, and she swung it toward her exasperated father. "It worked! It worked, Dad!" she screamed.

Bob was dumbfounded with the success of the "face", but he knew better than to betray the true facts of the catch. "Why see . . . I told you it would work. Good job!" congratulated Bob. The smelt flopped into the pail, and Wendy handed the line to Bob.

"I need more bait, Dad" she petitioned with a quick check of her other pole. She scrambled onto the ground beside the second pole and scrunched her face into the usual and now well-practiced contortion.

"Don't forget the cross-eyes!" bellowed Bob with fresh bait in hand. As he strung the piece of carved fish onto the hook, he chanced to see Wendy's good luck face at work.

"Here's another one!" exclaimed Wendy jumping up to land the fish and swing the silvery prize into the hands of her father. Bob exchanged his baited pole for her smelt-bearing rod, and she promptly put the fresh line into the water.

The temperature, time, and the tide were in their favor now. Bob was amused by the thought that his daughter's face would ache this evening if she repeated her fish face enough times to fill her pail. "Hon, don't waste all your good fish faces today. You have the smelt fooled pretty good now." He had no sooner offered the suggestion than a third smelt dangled from the hook on its way to the pail. "You try to unhook this one, Wendy," encouraged her father. She had the sliver of vibrating fish quickly under foot. The child disengaged the barb from the fish's mouth, a free hand replaced her foot over the smelt, and it was dispatched into the pail. "Very well done, Young Lady!" complimented her father.

The first hour of waiting gave way to a delirious forty minutes of activity. They fished through the gradual secession of smelt strikes as the school meandered through their gauntlet. Two and a half hours into the fishing trip Bob announced, "Wendy, I think we have enough smelt to do some powerful bragging at home. What do you think?" he questioned.

"Yep! Wait 'til everyone sees this mess of fish. Jim won't believe that my fish face is better than his, but he will when he looks in my bucket," she proudly announced.

The walk to the car took on an air of celebration. Bob had a swagger to his step and Wendy skipped most of the way. The gear was stowed securely in the trunk, but the smelt were still in the bucket at Wendy's feet as she stood by the passenger's side door. When the trunk lid slammed shut, she rushed gleefully upon her father. "Thank you so much, Dad!" she cooed, nestling up to his bulky frame. She threw her arms outward from her petite frame. In spontaneous appreciation, she wrapped them around the midsection of her father. He brought her head to his chest. The world was perfect.

The afternoon sun heated the interior of the vehicle. Bob and Wendy rolled down the front windows. The fresh air, the dust, the noises, and the soft seats were welcomed to the riders. Bob had his left hand out of his window. There was a popping, drumming sound somewhere near the driver's side. "What was that?" asked Bob. "Did you hear that, Wendy?"

"You made that noise, Dad. Didn't you?" she puzzled. Her father was a prankster, and his reputation made her cautious. He had been right about the fish face, though.

"Thump! Thump! Drum, drum, click, click!"

"I'm not sure if that's the motor or something got stuck on our roof or under the car," surmised Bob as he slowed the car, listening intently.

"Gosh, Dad! Is something's wrong with the car?" ventured the child. She was more concerned now as the auto decelerated.

"It's probably something stuck under the chassis," drummed Bob. "I'll pull over and we can check." The car sputtered to a stop near a mailbox. There was a cut-out worn by the daily postal delivery near a roadside residence. "Why don't you check it for me, Fisher Lady Extraordinaire," delivered Bob with a majestic flair.

"Sure, Dad, I'll check," obliged Wendy as she lifted the handle and swung from the seat. She shut the door, backed up and surveyed the exterior of the car on her side. "I don't see anything over here, Dad," she reported. She had taken a post next to the mailbox at the cut-out.

"Honey, look under the car," commanded Bob from the driver's seat. The car continued to idle, and Bob saw her back up a few more paces and drop to her knees. Their catch of smelt still sat in water in the pail on the floor at the passenger's side. The water percolated with the vibrations and hum of the engine's idle. Bob nudged the car forward and away from the cut-out onto the highway.

"Hey? Where ya goin'?" yelled Wendy who popped onto her feet at the first forward movement of the family car.

"Got ya!" teased her father as he moved farther up the road. "I'll tell them I caught all the fish!" taunted Bob.

"That's not fair!" blurted the child with fear and anger. "You come back here!" Wendy's competitive drive supplanted her initial outburst as she ordered Bob to pick her up. The car halted its forward movement with its brake lights glaring in submission. The white surrender flag of the reverse lights brought the father to a reunion with the feisty daughter. Hopping into the seat, Wendy landed a forceful jab onto the right upper arm of her father. "You made me mad; you scared me!" defended the little girl.

"Sorry, Honey, but I couldn't resist giving you a start," rationalized Bob with a mild apology. He leaned over, kissed her on the forehead, put the car in drive and proceeded homeward.

"I'll probably never forget this," contemplated the child. "It was a great day. Don't you think so, Dad?"

"One of the very best, Wendy," smiled Bob, admiring the depth and diversity of Wendy's view of the world.

Chapter Seven

"A Treasure from the Sea"
"The Belief in Reel Fiction"

A tale flavored by
Judy Berger Woods and the children

Perhaps on one particular Saturday morning in York, when the breezes were absent and the harbor lacked breath, and perhaps on that July day in the 1970's, a warm front visited during the night and left the seacoast still and the water flat. What might a day of fishing with the Berger family have been like? Bob frequently took his brood out in the boat on Saturdays for a day of family fishing.

* * *

Bob Berger's anxiety mounted with just the thought of taking the four children onto the ocean by himself in the Eagle. The operations of the vessel were familiar to him, second nature, and just the way he wanted it with the children on board. All four of the Berger offspring were already adept at handling rod and reel, but the unexpected concerned Bob. The weather was cooperating with his plans so he plodded onward through breakfast, speaking with excitement about the fishing they would have this day.

A phone call momentarily relieved his nervousness. It was Matt Corey, who was now a charter fisherman; and he had some fishing news about what was running in the surf and in the open ocean. The men exchanged the usual brain-picking questions about the best tackle and baits to use on each species that were now feeding off-shore. Matt had friends and fellow captains who wanted his views on the gear and methods to use. The young man always sought the experience and opinion of Bob first, especially after the striper-inside-a-striper incident.

Bob rattled off a litany of suggestions to his friend. "Heck, Bob! You ought to run a 'bait and tackle' shop up here," advised Matt over the receiver.

A brief silence hopped awkwardly into the conversation. The pause occurred as Bob realized that what he had just shared with Matt could be used today with the kids. "Yeah! One day I might try that, Matt." Then almost as an afterthought to the fishing information, Bob added, "I'm getting ready to take the gang out for some blues."

"Man, it's a great day out there for that! Hardly any surf at all—just nice easy swells. . . . The ocean's almost flat, Bob," he reported.

An idea formed in Bob's brain like a seam of ice cracking on a pond. "Matt, are you doin' anything, today?"

"My slate is clean for most of the day," he responded with an audible smile that Bob detected in his voice. "Why?"

"I've been meaning to ask you if you wanted to go along on the Eagle. With the gang on board, I could use a mate," confessed Bob. It was an unusual invitation from Bob. A certain independence of character, especially around fishermen, was a mark of his reputation. This request did not, however, alter Bob's position in Matt's estimation. "Would you be free to make a run with me and the family today for a few hours?"

These plans and the question were greeted with some disbelief and a goodly amount of curiosity. "Did I hear that right?" badgered Matt. "Like, I would be guiding with Bob Berger!" He was not quite awestruck, but the delivery was spiced with flattery. On the other end of the conversation, Bob could sense that Matt was actually considering joining the family on this lovely July day.

"I . . . we would love to have you join us," Bob reiterated. Then, in a shot to his brood nearby, he added, "Right, kids?" Berger screamed the interjection toward his family with his head turned away from the receiver. The approval from the youngsters was unanimous, and Matt was taken aback by the responses.

"Uncle Matt is coming! Great! Yeah! Can we help steer the boat? I wanna fish with Uncle Matt?" Matt heard the voices and imagined the enthusiastic faces.

"Sure, Bob, I'll come along," he volunteered. They set up a meeting time and, for Matt, a "return to harbor time." He had some of his own family commitments later in the day.

The Berger children bounded from the car with unrestrained energy and darted straight for the boat and Uncle Matt. The shipmate arrived dockside ahead of the Bergers and stood guard aft of the Eagle. Quick, sharp orders from the car turned the children about, and each ran back to his father. Bob was bent into the trunk, removing gear, coolers, trash bags and extra, smaller sized Mae Wests. Matt witnessed the loading of the caravan and its embarkation as the line of small porters filed toward the docks carrying their rods and reels. At the rear, Bob struggled with towels, bags and miscellaneous tackle piled carefully atop the plastic lunch cooler.

Matt shook his head and yelled, "You've got all your ducks in a row, Bob!" The brood was well-behaved, and they boarded the vessel with an air of familiarity that came from time spent with their father along the waterfront and around fisher people. It was a colorful day; the children were arrayed in a plethora of varied colored tees, shorts, and jeans. The boys had opted for jeans, and the girls picked out their favorite worn shorts, "Ones they could 'ruin'," as Lois had put it.

It was with some trepidation that Judy approached the boat. On a previous trip, she had an opportunity to take the helm of the Eagle and steer it to a fishing spot. During that earlier excursion, she could not redirect her attention from the multicolored buoys as they danced before the bow. As she bulldozed the fourth set, Bob relieved her of her commission. Her exploits piloting the boat caused her to be "thrown overboard" so to speak. Bob had "grounded" young Judy for running over lobster pots on a "regular basis".

Everyone else scampered on board, but Judy waited, poised to step onto the gunwale. Bob saw her quandary. "Come on, Young Lady! Hop aboard!" he invited.

Yet she hesitated, remembering the customs and routines of the York docks and marinas, and she went to attention like a sailor coming off leave. "Permission to come aboard, Captain?" she requested.

Captain Bob and Mate Corey eyed one another with warm smiles. The father in Bob suddenly understood. "You will not be piloting this trip, Sailor, so you have permission to board," ordered her father with bravado, obvious enough for Judy to get the point.

Bob played the proud parent, buoyed by his offspring's presence on his boat and by the relaxing assistance of his first mate. Matt watched Bob maneuver the boat from the dock into the channel and out through the inlet. The smell of fuel was evident at the lower speeds; but, as they throttled up, the salt air took over and the fishing trip was underway.

Matt began to set up the rigs for the children as Bob guided the group south along the coast. Flocks of sea birds dove into the ocean less than a mile from shore, and Bob headed to meet them. "I'll finish that, Matt, if you'll take the helm!" petitioned Bob.

"Alright . . . sure, I didn't get to Robbie or Wendy, but Robbie wants to do his own," issued Matt. He strode toward the helm with the sure steps of a practiced actor walking on stage through a familiar part. The forward progress of the boat and the calm sea made the jaunt effortless. They switched roles with teamwork created out of ritual and rite. Captain and mate were interchangeable.

The children's rigs were baited with white squid cut into long triangles or bits of young mackerel filleted into strips. Small barrel sinkers weighted the morsels enough to drag them beneath the surface and allow the bait to drop into the feeding zone of the smallish, snapper blues. Matt eased the throttle back and coaxed the motor into near idle as the party approached the first colony of feeding birds. The children had seen this before and knew the meaning of the signs. Fish were beneath them feeding on shad and minnow or bunker.

Bob placed a fly rod, already rigged with a light colored Clouser minnow, into the rod holding trough under the gunwale. With the youngsters set to fish, Bob reached for his rig but hesitated. "Hey Matt, did you bring a rod?" he flung at his acting captain.

On being addressed, the guide twisted backward, his feet faced forward at the helm and his head turned toward Bob. His eyes, however, continued to watch the birds and the children. "Nah, I'd rather be watching the little guys work some magic," he offered to Bob. The boat never settled into neutral for Matt deftly prompted the motor into a smooth trolling velocity. The fisher children in the back simply dropped the lines into the smooth sea with an open bale. Bob moved confidently to lock the spool on each rod when it reached the appropriate depth. He busied himself with their lines. With their gear at a prescribed depth, the children awaited a strike.

Two solid strikes produced shrieks from his children, "I got one!" signaled Jim.

"Me too, Dad, I got a big one!" added Judy. The small rods bent, struggling with taut line and the invisible power at the hook end. The two gladiators danced with their unseen adversaries, ducking beneath one another at times to change sides as the fish darted in chaotic runs behind the boat. Their two siblings continued to fish during the excitement, but Bob moved to take their gear from them. These lines were in the path of the brother and sister duet. First Mate Berger feverishly reeled their lines onto the spools and out of the way of the fight ensuing in the water behind them. They seemed to understand that they too would have a turn at the ballet. Robbie and Wendy witnessed patiently as the parts played out. Jim bullied his fish on board without a net, but Judy grappled with her rod and reel. Unsure about securing the tackle with only her right hand, she now grasped it with both hands so as not to lose it. Bob saw her dilemma and volunteered his left hand to her struggle. He twirled the handle steadily bringing in line as his young daughter took the weight and power of the bluefish with both hands. Jim's beaming smile was soon joined by Judy's as she saw her fish brought aboard in the landing net. Now the dance was lighter, a tippy-toe, tap; it was freer and unencumbered by the pull and tug of the feral fish.

"We'll only keep these if you're going to eat them, okay?" directed Bob to the fishermen. Jim did not hesitate and his went into the live-well. Judy dutifully followed Bob's directions and succeeded in placing the netted fish carefully back into the sea. The smiles never left their faces. "Matt, the blues aren't tail striking! They're smacking the whole bait," reported Bob to Matt.

"There's a hungry school down there, Bob," appraised the young man. "It's a feeding frenzy, all right."

The crew worked in pairs at baiting, hooking, landing and releasing fish. The two and three pound juvenile bluefish exhilarated the youngsters. Bob kept eyeing his fly rod, hoping like one of his children to get in a few casts. The pace was frantic and sweat oozed from Bob's brow. He could not manage the time to get to his fly rod. Matt figured that he had the better part of the bargain. He was having just as much enjoyment watching them without any of the mess. Bob wore scales, bait and blood all over his clothes.

Then a large portion of the school of blues vanished, chasing the bait fish to some unseen region in the vast coastal sea. The birds too were gone with them. Two of the lines were in the boat and Robbie and Wendy had baited rods in the water. No fish had taken any bait for minutes. Matt was scanning the ocean for the birds, but he saw no surface activity. Two of the youngsters were chatting between themselves about their catches, munching sandwiches that they had taken from the cooler. Bob saw the lull as a trough in the swell of activity. He grabbed his fly rod from its mooring and began to quickly strip off line. He had thirty feet or so out on the deck when he announced to Matt, more so than to the children, "I might hook up with a straggler!"

With practiced precision, Bob swung the line off the deck into the Atlantic with a careful and fluid roll cast. He pealed out twenty more feet of line onto the surface of the quiet sea. Making one back flip before a forward false cast, he laid the minnow at drawn-line length on the water. Bob checked that there were no knots or tangles.

"Bob! Bob! Wendy has a fish on!" yelled Matt, breaking Bob's concentration in an instant. Robbie was already moving to port side to make way for his sister.

"I'm a little tired, Dad," pleaded Wendy as she shot a soulful glance back to her father. In response, he instinctively placed the butt end of his fly rod into a nearby chrome edged rod holder cut into the gunwale.

"Okay, Honey, we'll take this one together," promised Bob to his anxious daughter. He bowed beside her, placing his left hand under hers. Gently pumping against the tug of the fish, they worked the rod and reel and garnered the prey to the boat. As Bob reached toward port to fetch the net, he heard Matt stammering and raving behind them.

"No, no, no . . . Bob! Bob!" he pleaded as if someone stole some words from him.

"What are you blabbering about?" quizzed Bob, turning to look at Matt full-faced. He heard no response, but rather noticed Matt's right arm pointing to the starboard gunwale. He followed the point but took no notice to anything that might produce such a reaction from his friend.

"Your fly rod's gone!" he snapped. It gushed outward as if it were a bottled up carbonated beverage that had suddenly been pried open. "I saw it bend with a hard strike. The recoil popped it up into the air. It just, like kinda, jumped into the ocean, Bob." He said it resolutely with sympathy, for he sensed that it was a brand new rod and reel.

"Cut the engine!" shot Bob. Obediently, his captain threw the gears into neutral, and the boat eased to a drifting float. Simultaneously, Bob netted Wendy's fish with one hand and directed Matt with hand gestures from the other. In a calm decisive manner, Bob took control of the chaos that sprung upon him.

"I did, but . . . why?" befuddled Matt with two open palms jutting outward toward the stern of the craft and to the passengers.

"We've got one line in the water—Robbie's," he tossed toward Matt and then to his son, "Let it settle to the bottom,

Robbie." Bob commanded the actions like a field general making adjustments to a plan run amok.

"Then what?" came the retort from his captain.

"Then, we'll run as slowly as possible, dragging the weight and hook of Rob's line on the bottom. Just make a slow arcing turn toward starboard. Maybe we'll snag my gear," envisioned Bob in a prayer to his friend, the children, and the air about him.

"Right!" delivered Matt, and the babble of the engine throated itself into a creeping troll. They had no time to check coordinates, but Bob looked landward, hoping to spot some familiar landmark by which to navigate the recovery of his lost gear.

"That was a spanking new Thomas and Thomas fly rod and an Islander reel, Matt. I just picked them up as a lightweight saltwater set. I figured I could use them for pike and bass in freshwater, too." He was reminiscing more than conversing with his companion. During the proceedings, which the children witnessed with respectful silence, they followed the adult's concern etched onto Uncle Matt's visage.

"I hope this . . ." began Matt, but something cut him off in mid sentence. He turned from Bob when he detected, peripherally, an odd movement on his port side. "No! Robbie's got a fish on," bemoaned Matt. "That'll ruin any chances of retrieving your gear."

"Maybe it's my rod—not a fish!" wished Bob with growing impatience.

"What do you think, Robbie?" asked Uncle Matt. The question caught the lad off guard. He was not prepared to offer an opinion on the situation. Now, he was a reluctant participant. Within him, turmoil boiled—he wanted to give his father hope, but the fish on the line spoke a different truth to him.

"It could be your rod, Dad . . . but I thought I felt it pounding like a fish," he surmised.

"That could be my rod dragging along the bottom, Son," hoped Bob. In another minute, the truth became visible. Darting left and right in the water at the aft of the boat, a fish made hard, desperate runs to avoid capture.

49

Matt dropped the boat into neutral and walked astern to lend assistance to Robbie. Uncle Matt netted his fish, but Bob was too disgruntled to display any joy in the landing of the bluefish. Defeated, he slumped in retreat off to the port side on the deck with his legs drawn into his chest. His arms rested on his knees, and his head was hung in submission to the whims of fate. The three other children gathered around the net next to Matt and Robbie. Matt emptied the net onto the deck. The four children and lone adult surveyed the catch. Bob wanted no part of it, for it had taken his last hope from him.

It was Judy who spoke through the silence with a gentle observation. "Uncle Matt, how come this fish has two hooks in his mouth?" No one ventured any comment, but there on the deck was a bluefish with volumes to speak.

"Hey! Who was fishing with mackerel?" pondered Uncle Matt.

"I am, Uncle Matt," admitted young Robbie who knelt reverently by his catch to examine the curiosity. The fish lay still on its side with one bulging eye scowling into the face of its captor. Robbie touched the second bait and announced, "This guy has a white buck tail in him, too."

Bob found nothing of interest in the conversation between Robbie and Matt until he heard "white." Just then Bob aped, "White?" He stirred from his retreat, rising from the deck, hungry for another chance.

Matt joined Robbie at the side of the oddity and, swept up by adulthood, began instructing the youth on the variations of fishing lures. "Robbie! That is not a buck tail. That's a Clouser minnow."

Bob wedged into their company, prompted by hope and urged onward by some unnamed competitive drive. He wanted some small victory over fact, fate, and the sea. He pushed his way into the center of his crew. The younger children ceded their positions to their father hoping the oddity of the bluefish might alleviate his torment. Bob touched the fly, felt its moistness, removed it from its prison in the fish's mouth and addressed it with the reverence usually afforded a sacred relic. "You, you wonderful fly, you are attached to my rod and reel! Aren't you?" With that prayer, he stood with the fly between thumb and index finger and the terminal leader in hand and began to jubilantly salvage, hand over hand, his new and recently lost fly fishing gear.

The children, like expectant parents awaiting the arrival of Dad's equipment from the briny deep, stood captive by the moment. Soon the rod tip appeared, and their father's elation infected them. Then the ferules surfaced, pulsing to-and-fro, but the gear refused to come aboard. The skirmish ended when the midpoint of the rod was grasped firmly in Bob's right hand and hoisted onto the Eagle. With no learned ritual for such an event, the children and men celebrated with an impromptu series of hugs, hand slaps, and various exclamations of jubilation.

Bob caught a glimpse of the bluefish flitting about on the deck. The death pangs of the captured fish took Bob from his festive mood. Placing the rod securely under the gunwale, he strode toward the three pound bluefish. Matt imagined Bob was descending a flight of three steps, for each succeeding pace brought Bob lower and lower toward the deck. He stopped alongside the fish, kneeling on his right knee. "Kids," he summoned, "This fellow here is going back. Don't you think he did me a big favor hitting Robbie's mackerel after grabbing my fly?" He received nods of consent from the Berger family, and a "Do what you want" wave from Matt. Bob tailed the fish and, rather than toss it indifferently into the water, the young bluefish was lowered reverently into the swirling eddies beyond the transom. "I hope we meet again!" he invited. The flash of sleek blue and silver responded with a spray of salt water as the fish flung one last tail swipe back toward the Eagle.

The return trip with the vessel went without incident. *Red Right, Returning* echoed in Bob's mind as he navigated the tidal wash and the delta run-out from the York River. Matt minded his progress but not a word needed to be spoken. The children were quiet: fatigue becalmed them. Bob appreciated the stillness which allowed him to concentrate on his piloting tasks.

Lashed to the slip, the boat rested quiet and secure. Bob started toward Matt, but the prey recognized his stalking gait.

Matt was stepping backward with hands buffering the approach of Bob. Reluctantly, he permitted the friendly thanks and the fishy aura of Bob's arms around him.

Bob knew that, when the children's feet hit the dock, they would be rejuvenated. The afternoon cookout with clams and the few bluefish that they had culled from the Atlantic would quickly become the anticipated delight of the day. They left the dock, scurrying to tell their stories of a day of fishing with Dad and Uncle Matt.

Chapter Eight

"The Lure of the Green Links"
"Some Fables Are Real Fiction"

*A myth, flavored in part by Arthur Berger
and Richard McCleod and embossed by
David Sowerby and William Mitchell
with whom the author played golf and fished.*

The children grew and the "Sons" actually took up their labor from time to time at the garage. Bob had a little more free time for hunting, snowmobiling, fishing and golf. Lois and Bob were parting ways, but the family was held together by values, respect, and those cookouts. Bob took in what life had to offer and remained ever eager, able, and willing to participate. His lifestyle was the envy of the men of York. The Berger golf lore recounted his solid handicap, his low running draw, his passion for the links, and his golf bag nestled in any vehicle in which he travelled.

The York Golf and Tennis Club rests on the east side of the York River and not far from its mouth. Many of the Mainers who frequent the club are families long associated with the community. The club does have a small clique of newer members who generally share their interests in fitness, politics and economics with the vested members. They do not, however, share their history.

Bob received an invitation to join some members one weekday for a round of golf. As a youth, he took an interest in the game well before boot camp. Some of his fellow GIs had a liking for the sport, and Bob continued to play out of curiosity. He realized that the time on any course became a social event, and that was a favorable aspect of the game for Bob. With better-than-average hand and eye coordination, Bob managed to evolve into a passable player, eventually carrying a ten handicap.

Some of the Sowerbys and Mitchells had joined The York Golf and Tennis Club, and they entertained their fellow members with tales of Robert Berger. Art Berger was also a member; and that, along with the stories of Bob's fishing exploits, was grounds enough for an invitation to play "The Club." His presence in any foursome promised to add interest to the match. A foursome was arranged through Dick McCleod, the professional, and Bob was set to play.

The two older members who were part of the foursome were affable and relaxed gentlemen. Charlie Shoemaker was lean and narrow, and his pace and carriage resembled a jogger rather than a sprinter. Greg McLaughlin, Sr., had a rounded profile that projected a shadow that matched Bob's when they stood side by side. Both Charlie and Greg were retired from business, and their interests and conversation drifted from the stock market and politics toward the more mundane. They cherished diversions of all sorts. Cards, golf, some fishing, dining and couple-functions pocked their calendars with events meant to draw them from lassitude and ennui.

Bob sensed that there were certainly things to be learned here. Sometimes, when he guided strangers on a trip, he noticed this same comportment. He recognized the particular needs of retired persons. This made him more valuable to his clientele, and he constantly improved his people skills by his keen observations. As a nymph going through natural transformation, Bob's experiences honed his skills and prepared him for life as an adult. By listening, Bob was learning to say what people wanted to hear and to reach them through their own backyards.

The third member of the York Country Club contingent was John Mayer, a younger man whose energy contrasted the two older companions. His wavy, jet black hair had just begun to salt-and-pepper. He was reluctant to leave the business and political topics and appeared sullen when Shoemaker and McLaughlin swung those focal points toward hobbies and entertainment. Bob felt like the mediator during the initial jousting that moved the men from parking lot, through locker room, and into the small functional Pro Shop.

Dick McCleod, appropriately dressed in golf attire embossed with muted logos of the club, chatted politely with the group. The professional managed to give Bob a brief introduction, a preview as it were, into the lives of his members before sending the foursome to the first tee. Bob learned that John worked with bankers and investors. He formed a group of entrepreneurs who were eager to expend capital on small risk, upstart businesses, especially restaurants. John's eyes glistened with his passion for the competitive world of finance. Bob was taking some serious mental notes.

The approach to the tee from the club house was an awkward one. Attached to an unfamiliar golf pull-cart, Bob yanked the beast a few strides with his left arm, and then shifted to a right hand grip. Generally, his fellow golfers rode in electric or gas carts, unencumbered by the awkward weight of golf bags stuffed with long shafted clubs and dozens of golf balls.

The first tee alongside the club house presented a clear, unobstructed vista of the first hole. Bob liked starting with a par three even though its length measured two hundred and fifteen yards. Visually, it offered no particular difficulty for the foursome as its wide fairway ran straight to a tilted, large green. After their first shots, Bob and the others pulled their wares like reluctant buckboard mules from the first tee toward the green. A bogie on the first hole left Bob more settled with his newly drawn friends. He shoved a wad of chewing tobacco into his cheek. John was "given" Bob as partner by default, as the two elder statesmen opted to play together.

"Pulling this cart gives a different feel to the game. Do you pull or push it?" posed Bob to his playing companion.

"Whichever you like, Bob! It took me awhile to get used to," contributed John as he manipulated his equipment. He foraged in his right pocket for a tee and his Titleist. Backing up a pace, he placed his putter in the bag and selected his driver. "The club where I played in New York had electric carts. It seems to be a tradition at quite a few New England private clubs to use pull-carts." His younger partner carried the lowest handicap of the group, and Bob found John's abilities to be an asset to his round. Help came from John's experience, lessons that he had taken from McCleod, and his cool deliberation.

The chaw of tobacco in Bob's mouth became unruly and awkward. His covert dropping of the morsel into the trash canister at the seventh tee box improved his concentration and added to the social decorum of the private country club. Shoemaker and McLaughlin nearly played to their handicaps, and the Berger-Mayer twosome found it challenging to stay all-square by the end of nine holes. Bob registered an honest forty-four on the par thirty-five front. His team's adjusted composite score equaled the competition at net thirty-seven.

The senior pair reveled enough in their golf fortunes to pick up the food tab at the turn. Like many a member golfer, the two wily veterans looked for an edge against their opponents on the back nine. With the growth of the new friendships that surfaced during the front nine, Bob merely hoped for a tie as the outcome.

After teeing off on the three hundred and ninety-one yard tenth tee, the older Shoemaker inquired, "Say, Bob? You're a Korean Vet, right?"

"Yep," returned as Bob's subtle affirmative. It left a brassy flavor on his tongue. Bob stood off the tee awaiting John's effort and feigned a pretext of concentrated focus on his partner's upcoming drive.

The senior McLaughlin took up the investigation when the short response left his partner befuddled. "I guess you saw a lot of action?" he added.

"Yep," came back almost as a courtesy. The word swung from Bob simultaneously with the metallic "click" from John's big headed driver. Berger bit his lower lip and reflected . . . *Got me yapping during John's swing.* Bob picked up on their two pronged attack. His remedy was to slow down his gait, his breathing, his movements and his thoughts. He would not permit, in his own defense, any such musings to violate the present time. The Korean War veteran sought refuge in the brevity of his answers. Those combat days he chose to keep in dusty storage somewhere. Bob was not about to unlock those events or rustle up the missing mental key. The obligation to be sociable still pushed the "on" button, bringing an unpleasant taste into his mouth.

"Did you ever catch something really unexpected, Bob?" interrupted John as he strode off the tee. It stirred Bob from his momentary downshift. He was pleased with the question, for it offered a new perspective, different from the path of the earlier interrogatives.

"Fishing *is* the unexpected, but . . . yes, I did!" he pitched. A twinkle sprung into his eyes, and lightness etched his words. "And my children were witnesses."

The older gentlemen had heard this narrative from Sowerby and Mitchell, but now they were captivated by the events as only Bob could tell them. They were thrown off their gambit, as it lost its importance in the tale of how Robbie's hungry bluefish had salvaged Bob's rod and reel. John and Bob came together like an alloy, two distinct individuals who strengthened the properties of the other. Bob worked his magic.

Stories cascaded from the foursome, but it was the offer by John which left its mark on Bob. Their futures became the subject, and Bob sowed his vague plans and aspirations into the conversation of the foursome like kernels awaiting the arrival of potting soil. "Someday, Bob, when you're ready to test your hand at a bait shop, let me know. Maybe I can help you out?"

On the sixteenth, par four, Greg McLaughlin, put his ball into a lateral water hazard. He busied himself fumbling for his ball retriever with its telescoping shaft. Checking down the fairway, he noted that no other group was close upon them. He appeared doggedly determined to rescue the ball, for the retriever was extended to its full length. He caught sight of Bob rummaging about at his bag and figured that some added assistance was forthcoming. He started to address Bob, "Well, thanks for the . . ." Caught off his guard, McLaughlin was startled into silence by the image that his eyes sent to his disbelieving brain.

Bob held the top-half of a fishing pole in his right hand. He was unfurling line from its loops around the ferrules. At the end of braided line was a feathery tidbit with a metallic glimmer. Bob barely heard McLaughlin's words, for he was intent on his own foraging. Both John and Charlie sauntered over beside Bob. It was obvious to them that Bob was not fishing for golf balls. He slapped the fly onto the water as if to awaken the denizens of the pool. "Heh, Heh!" he giggled, "Got one!" A small bream dangled surprised from the end of his line. It twitched rapidly, raining water from its soaked body. "Take your time retrieving your ball, Greg," suggested Bob. "I might be able to get a little 'smallie' out of here!" His voice carried an emotion thrilled by his discovery of fish on the course.

"Charlie?" shot McLaughlin, "you remember that tape of Dave Archer, the golf pro, spin casting after his round down in Florida?" It was his memory, but it admitted him into the fishing club on the sixteenth fairway.

"Sure, he'd catch a slew of big bass right after his competitive round," contributed Charlie, still standing by Bob. "Look here, Greg. He's got a smallmouth bass alright," celebrated Charlie, now caught up in the moment.

"Got it!" stammered Greg. All heads turned to him expecting to see a fish dangling from his retriever. They had forgotten golf. A white sphere rested in the oval cup at the end of the long shaft. Mc Laughlin read their faces and the disappointment when they saw the ball. "We had better not tie up the course," suggested the player as he flung the ball to the ground and prepared to play it. "I don't want to slow us down any more by taking the distance penalty. Is it okay with you guys if I just play it here?" he petitioned.

John held a wide grin on his joy-filled face. He slapped Bob firmly on his right shoulder and reluctantly returned to his cart. "That's nuts!" he exclaimed, still beaming widely. "I've never golf-fished before."

Laughter accompanied the group up the sixteenth. Rumbles of amusement re-occurred on the seventeenth and eighteenth also. Charles Shoemaker won the match for his team on the last hole with a bending twelve footer for a birdie. John could not hold back the child in him as he joked, "We should call that putt a 'fishie'!" He sprang at his partner, shook his right hand and threw his left arm around the stocky Bob Berger. They held that habit in common, for Bob too was about to embrace his newest friend.

Bob was informed that he now owed Greg McLaughlin three dollars as his contribution from the losing team to the victors. John took care of the team debt to Charlie.

During his life in York, Maine, Robert Berger added significantly to its lore. It was easy for him—fame or rather notoriety settled upon him as a natural accessory to his life. The Bergers did briefly join the York Golf and Tennis Club, but Bob played enough rounds there with his brother and other members that the professional, Dick McCleod, began to believe he was a permanent full member. Bob found The Cliffs Country Club near York Village to be more affordable, and the Berger family became long-standing members there.

A close friend, Ferris Boardman, remembered a round of golf at The Cliffs with Bob. The lanky, dark haired Mainer and two of his companions left Bob at the bar after their eighteen holes. The bourbon was particularly enjoyable that afternoon, for Bob deserted his friends in exchange for finishing his drink. Ferris watched the two fellows reconnoiter Bob's Saab. They busied themselves with hurried antics at their autos and at Bob's. They inspected the front end and appeared to perform some minor repairs to the undercarriage. As they returned to Ferris at the front of the club, Bob exited the building. Brief cordial goodbyes ensued and Ferris received a bourbon perfumed hug. Finally in his Saab, Bob turned the ignition, started the auto, and clutched into first gear. The Saab roared but no movement accompanied the purr of the engine. Second gear was tested. Then Bob shifted into third gear with a loud whine that muffled the uproarious laughter from the two pranksters at the clubhouse. In neutral, the truth finally dawned upon Bob. He exited the idling auto, thrust a frustrated and embarrassed left arm in the direction of the mischievous golf partners, and threw his right hip solidly into the front left fender of the Saab. The car listed right and bobbled on firm ground off of the two jacks that had rested under the front-wheel drive vehicle. Bob mumbled some unheard epithets into his front windshield as he drove off. Rolling peals of laughter echoed from The Cliffs Country Club.

Bob honed his techniques in fly fishing: instructing, guiding and crafting flies. He became proficient with the tools of the fisherman's art. Youngsters like Adam DeBruin and young Joe Sowerby found in him a valuable mentor. The new Mainers learned to love the water and the blessings it granted to those who sought its grandeur and complexity. The calm and the storm, the feast and the famine, and the joy and the pain were to be experienced to their fullest. Those willing to put time and energy into their lives with Bob Berger's example were soon rewarded.

Florida lured him magnetically throughout the rearing of his children, his marriage, his subsequent divorce, and his numerous friendships. After his marriage ended and his children grew into adulthood, a comfortable freedom to wander with the seasons invaded him. He met a wonderful companion in Jan Wood at the Spice of Life Restaurant in York. She meshed easily with his lifestyle, enjoying the travel and the diversions.

Bob sought out golf courses to play all along his travel routes. He fished every available opportunity in a myriad of waterways: ponds, streams, rivers, and lakes and bays, cuts, flats, oceans, and seas. Bob Berger chased the trout on the Madison in Montana and the salt water sport fish in the Florida Keys. He embraced with passion the freedom deeply rooted in his being, spicing his life with purpose.

Chapter Nine

"The New Swimming Hole"

As told in part by Wendy Berger Rogers,
Jan Wood, Richard Mitchell, William Coite,
David Sowerby, and William "Ledge" Mitchell

During the harsh winter seasons of hibernation along the Maine coastline, Bob formulated a plan, a dream to extend his love of angling into the entire year. Bob was usually infected with "cabin fever" by Thanksgiving. The hunting trips and snowmobiling jaunts, which provided some needed cleansing with fresh, brisk air, were fleeting and infrequent. The urge to drink amply of life and the coaxing of the mystique of Florida whetted his desire to shower in its fullness.

Beginning in 1981, Bob began his annual migration to the Florida Keys. He settled in Islamorada and took a seasonal job at Chittums in sales. One of the other employees, Chet Pryor, struck up a familiarity with Bob, and they became close friends. The two spent time fishing and playing cribbage.

Then, in 1985, Jan journeyed with him to Islamorada in response to winter's cruel and imposed hiatus from the summer's short-sleeved outdoor life. A decade his junior she possessed an energetic freckled face that warmly glowed with a fun-loving smile. She carried her buxom figure well, and the "Doris Day" image she conveyed endeared her to everyone. By now they were staying year round at motels and cabins. Finally, the couple settled into a mobile home off Route One on Upper Matecumbe Drive.

The Fourth of July weekend in 1985 brought Wendy to Islamorada for a visit. For the holidays and summer months, Chittums's store hours were abbreviated and Chet and Bob were sharing duties. This arrangement afforded Bob and Wendy time to spend together. As her brother Jim, she had taken up residence in Florida. That tenure would last for six years before she returned to Maine.

Anne's Beach was crowded and buzzed with the noises and activities of families and friends. The majority of sun worshipers camped on the strand near the channel cut by the receding tide. The water was deeper there. Bob and Wendy set up their squatter's towels on the fringe of the festive bathers on the north side of the sandy tract. Bob smoothed his blanket, set up a low-slung lawn chair and moved his cooler alongside his gear. He watched Wendy prepare her own comfort zone and then apply sunscreen before lying belly-down on her blanket.

"So, Wendy, you say Jim's doing well with the business," exhaled Bob in a relaxed, soft delivery that was carefree.

"Yes, he is," she stressed all three words as a guarantee of her truthful assessment. "The family and the business are both doing well. They like Dania Beach."

"Good! I'm glad for him. It's always a risk working in the yacht business," philosophized Bob as he opened the cooler. "You want a beer or a soda?"

"Not right now Dad, but you go ahead," invited his daughter. She turned onto one side facing Bob and watched him draw a whiskey glass from the plastic tub. "Oh, you must have brought some Jack Daniels?"

"Well, Hon', I'm still trying to ease the pain from that cribbage shellacking you gave me last night," bemoaned Bob, dropping several ice cubes into the empty class. The unopened fifth of JD appeared. Bob twisted the cap and poured the liquid ceremoniously onto the ice until the level forced the ice to float.

"You still measure your drink by the buoyancy test, huh, Dad?" observed Wendy.

His answer was a simple nod of the head and a wink of his right eye. Bob raised his glass to her in an unspoken toast and took his first sip of his favorite Tennessee Bourbon. After savoring the first swallow, he reflected, "It's nice that you get a chance to see Jim and me while you're living down here."

"And I can't wait to tell Jim about the skunking I put on Mr. Expert last night!" challenged Wendy with a tinge of pride and elation.

Bob eased the glass to his lips and peered over the rim at his daughter. "You're not going to let me live that one down, are you?" he figured.

"That's right! The whole world's going to hear about it, Maine to Montana to Florida," egged Wendy to the profile of her father as he stared out into the vast blueness before him.

"I'll just tell everyone that you cheated," he countered. "No one will believe that you whooped me." Another sip of whiskey followed his defensive maneuvering.

"We'll see, Dad," teased Wendy. "I've already sent out some postcards with the news."

"I guess I'm about to lose my World Class Ranking. I'll probably drop to number three or something," bewailed Bob.

"Now, you know who's '*Numero Uno*'!" she exclaimed. "Wendy Berger!"

The afternoon slithered along toward a western sun. Wendy served some sandwiches and potato salad with conversations about family, friends, fishing memories and their mutual lives. Bob added inventory to her collection of Dad stories, but he was prudent about which ones would travel well with her on her rounds of visits. He confessed to missing the tide off Pompano Beach. He put his boat onto a sandbar. "Damn things are worse than snowdrifts!" he exclaimed. "I got back in pitch dark. Jan was atilt and worried sick at the same time. I bought her off and cooled her down with a nice batch of fresh, well, kinda fresh, yellow tails."

Wendy enjoyed his nearness, his sharing and the deep breaths with which he inhaled life.

Near to five o'clock, Bob reached into the cooler and checked his fifth of Jack Daniels. A good one-third was missing. He gently returned it to the cooler and made an effort to push himself from his beach chair. "Umph, shoot!" spat Bob as he toiled to remove himself from the low seat. Wendy smiled at his clumsy exertion, for she knew he had imbibed more whiskey than a warm afternoon permitted. Bob met her attempt to arise and assist him with a waist-high wave that held her at bay. An awkward hip thrust from Bob followed. It drove him forward onto his knees and placed him in the sand in front of his chair.

"Good Bourbon, huh Dad?" she quizzed ironically. She had no idea of Bob's plans until he proceeded to empty his pocket of keys and wallet. "You're going in the water?"

"Yeah! Is that okay with you Miss-Smarty-Pants?" queried Bob, for he had understood her "Bourbon" comment. "Just gonna freshen up a bit," he danced the last words at her with gyrations like a man in a shower rinsing off the sand of the beach.

She laughed as she followed his amble into the water of Anne's Beach. The crowds had diminished, and only splotches of bathers and walkers were along the beach. Bob's ship was far from being on an even keel. He listed to port with a more pronounced waddle and swing than usual. His head bent forward aiming himself at the ocean. Reaching for his waist with both hands, he pulled up his sagging fishing shorts, aka swim trunks. Wendy followed him into the water with watchful attention, amused at the boyishness of her father. His Bourbon spoke through him in a symphony of odd motions, painting him with a gentle awkwardness. His bulky frame became a flag waving in a steady, soft breeze. She left him to his play when she picked up a magazine.

Sometime later, her reading was disturbed by the splashing and slapping of a bather exiting the warm Atlantic. Before she looked up, she heard grunts and groans. Then a distinct, "Oh, shit!" was audible from the shoreline. Wendy's eyes flipped upward and fell into focus on a bewildered, roundish man with a sopping wet beard. The motions of her father momentarily drew Wendy's attention from his appearance. Bob's bushy beard was transformed into a dripping, gray-white wet mop. Frantically, he swung about searching the sand around him. Pirouetting at the water's edge was her father scanning the water for his fishing shorts, the lost swim trunks.

Holding her broadly grinning mouth closed with both of her hands, Wendy muted the laughter that fought to leap into the afternoon air. The young woman sat immobile and transfixed by the scene before her. Fortunately, Bob wore boxer shorts under his fishing shorts, but they were wetted almost transparent by the ocean water. Finally, Wendy managed to call out, "Did you lose something?" The words were chased quickly by the uproarious laughter freely gushing from her.

"Don't say another thing, Young Lady!" commanded Bob who, at that point, gave up his futile search. He wheeled about and stormed toward their beach position. "I know I'm never going to live this one down either." When his shadow reached her, he was already gathering the beach towel about himself. With sober decorum, Bob garnered enough control of himself to exit the beach, carrying his paraphernalia without any apparent ill effects from his afternoon of Bourbon drinking.

Wendy chatted ceaselessly as she hurried after her retreating father. He tossed her the car keys along the way and found no humor in her joy-filled face and grinning mouth. "How'd you let them float away? Were you sleeping when you were floating? Boy! The rest of the gang's going to love this story! Did you take them off? Or did they get snagged on something out there?"

Bob would not answer any of her questions or acknowledge any of the comments. Upon reaching the car, he turned toward Wendy, put down the gear he was lugging, and secured the towel firmly about his trunk. Bob opened his arms inviting an embrace. Finally, while holding his daughter, he spoke, "I don't know how I lost my drawers, but I know you're going to have some fun with this one."

"Yep, you won't live it down, Dad, and thanks," she added.

"Thanks?" he retaliated with sarcasm into the top of her head.

"Sure, you have filled my life with such awesome memories! I doubt any other daughter had a Dad like you. You're one in a million!" she beamed, giving him one last fierce clutch in their embrace before stepping away. Bob darted into the car draped in his beach towel. Wendy loaded the trunk with the picnic items and took the helm.

"Okay Mate, take us north by northwest and hold that setting!" played Bob.

"Aye, aye, Captain!" returned Wendy, entering into the wonderful world of Bob Berger.

* * *

Bob continued to work at Chittums and flourished as a customer service agent. He sometimes appeared to be socializing more than working, but his supervisors knew that he was bringing in much repeat business. Those early scouting forays into business and fishing with Chet allowed Bob to test the waters and learn the skills needed to fish the Keys. He did purchase the Chris Craft from Ledge's father and piloted it down into Islamorada from Ocean Reef. The fisherman studied the multiple species of fish, their habits, their likes and dislikes; and he practiced his trade. Locals gave him valuable information about the possibility of opening a fly shop and what might be the best wares to sell. Bob was already attached to the older rods and antique reels. Winston, Islanders, and the Thomas and Thomas gear suited his fancy; and he began collecting them with a keen business eye.

In some speculative conversations with John Mayer and locals in the Keys, Bob developed a business scenario which accommodated his life style. He decided to open a fly fishing shop in the Keys of Florida based upon his ability to guide, his experience as a hard-working small businessman, and his driven self-confidence. Banks moved slowly in their approval of such a venture. Acting independently of others was more to his demeanor. He terminated any "feelers" with John, with the banks, and with any of the locals who had given him advice. All these plans were held in abeyance until he would take up permanent residence in 1991. When it happened, it would be Robert E. Berger's business.

The old adage, "Location, Location, and Location," dominated the research and led to his scouting Islamorada for the most likely spot to drop anchor and start a business. It was generally touted as "The Sport's Fishing Capital of the World", and Bob knew that he could supply an unusual bent to the fishing knowledge of this salt water paradise. In 1992, scouring the real estate of the Keys, Bob settled on a small property at 81900 Overseas Highway that was no more than a low-slung store front tucked into the middle of a strip mall. It shared the parking lot with Sunny Exposures, a women's boutique, and the Ichthyophile, an arty shop dealing with all aspects of fish.

The storefront's individuality was marked by an enormous eight foot bow window resting on its cinder block support wall. Large panes of eighteen-inch square glass panels, set four high, let the morning sun into the display area in front of the shop. Bob kept the place cleanly white with an azure blue trim. That color also decorated the front door to the left of the bow window. An American flag pointed to the rising sun on the corner strut of the bow. As if to inform little children and adults of the establishment's name, Bob had "Bonefish Bob's, Ye Old Tackle Shop" emblazoned below and above the store front window. He put up a message board of sorts on the right side of the door at eye-level. It often read like a menu, featuring data on fishing conditions, gear, locations of bonefish, personal messages, and sales items.

As fate would have it, Jan and he moved to 74 Lower Matecumbe Drive, just a walking distance from his shop. Routinely, on his way most mornings, he stopped for his usual breakfast of freshly prepared oatmeal and a few cups of tea at the pastry shop.

Bonefish Bob's had gulf-side access with a rickety little boat ramp down the side alley. The incline jutted some thirty feet into deeper water. Some earlier occupant dredged the coral bottom sufficiently to allow for deeper hulled boats to be moored. After the demise of the Chris Craft, Bob kept his Hewes flats boat, a john boat, and, some people even reported, a yellow kayak docked there.

His wealth of fishing experience complemented his business savvy. The garage trained him well in inventory size, variety of stock and displays. His story-telling nature, his gentle and friendly manner, the charitable gift of his time, and his sincerity with his clients made Bonefish Bob's only a small risk as a business venture.

Before his statehood changed its affiliation to Florida, the time spent with the younger fishermen of York had begun to show results. His fledglings, Dave Sowerby's son, Joe, and Adam DeBruin, both became capable guides and businessmen working year round with their craft. Joe eventually drifted to Montana and opened his own guide service, Montana Flyfishing Connection in Missoula. After graduating from Humboldt State University in Northern California, Adam went to work for Joe on four and six day float trips. He eventually worked his way to the Keys during the winter months. Adam brought many of the Montana guides down to Florida including Steve Blanche and Kirk Gammill. Bob took them under wing in exchange for cribbage and chess games. There were always pegs in the cribbage board and a chess game in progress in Bonefish Bob's, Ye Old Tackle Shop.

Family and friends from the North visited the Keys to spend time with Bob, and they came down to rest, relax, and assimilate the mystique of Bonefish Bob. Harold Sussman visited on occasions from Maine with others from York. One day some locals who arrived to pick up supplies found Harold trashing the store. His practical joke left the locals speechless as they watched Bob and Harold laughing, teasing, and picking the wares of the shop off the floor and replacing the items on their respective shelves. The unexpected was Bonefish Bob's delight. To Harold and locals, Robert E. Berger became "Bonefish Bob" and "BFB" appeared on his tee-shirts.

Visitors were numerous and always welcomed. Art Berger and his wife would fly into Islamorada's local airstrip to fish, golf and vacation. Bob always picked them up, happy to see them and anxious to have them enjoy his world. Bob usually teased Art's wife unmercifully in exchange for her endless badgering of him. The favorite ice-breaker for Bob was always the same, and it was dreaded by Mrs. Berger. On the way to the small airport, Bob would get an enormously large chew of tobacco working in his mouth. He made sure that some drivel oozed onto his beard and moustache. For his brother, Bob's greeting was a rib crushing embrace, but, to the proper Misses,

Bob landed a full mouthed kiss spiced by tobacco juice. Art was dumbfounded that the two pranksters still managed to share a peaceful and warm relationship. Mrs. Berger eventually prepared herself for such antics by carrying disposable wipes in easy reach within her handbag. The Art Bergers and Jan and Bob would fish the Atlantic side in the morning and switch to the gulf for the afternoon. The foursome also played golf and put relaxation to the forefront of their keys-style get-away, bedecked in their free BFB tee-shirts.

Those tees had another fame attached to them. On occasion, while standing outside the Ichthyophile shop next door, Rich Mitchell, the owner, sometimes saw the tell-tale flash of a Polaroid camera shoot from Bonefish Bob's front window. Giggling women would soon leave the shop carrying a BFB tee-shirt draped over their arms. Rich learned that Bonefish Bob had a collection of photos of these ladies. They apparently exchanged a Mardi Gras-style topless picture for one of Bob's treasured BFB tees.

Throughout those initial seasons, however, like any business in its infancy, Bonefish Bob's struggled with inventory, displays, gear company contracts and Bob's guiding. The locals were suspicious of a newcomer, especially if his presence impinged on their own guiding profits and sales' margins. The edge that Bob possessed was "Bob". He made friends easily and continued to bring people quickly into his comfort zone.

Bob befriended a local fisherman, Greg Theiman, who was down on his luck. He clerked at the shop with Chet Pryor which gave Bob some extra free time for lunches and fishing during shop hours. Bob had the eccentric habit of closing the shop for long lunches down at Steve's Time Out Bar-B-Q south of the shop. Greg or Chet stayed with the shop if it had to remain open at a particular lunch hour, but he frequently locked up shop for lunch.

Steve's was a haunt of local guides and few tourists. It reminded Bob of a palm tree encircled version of Norma's Kitchen, and both nestled within eye, ear, and nose recognition of the Atlantic Ocean. The fishermen frequenting this diner south of Bob's shop often introduced themselves to him with the question, "Oh! So you're Bonefish Bob?" They were hooked, and Bob's presence in Islamorada began to nudge into the life of the village.

Profits kept a low profile, but Bob worked hard those first few years to earn some financial stability. At a minimum, Bob wanted to break even, for the rise of Bonefish Bob's was not intended to be the high-end financial success that others might have expected. In the end, Bob had his own business and joyfully embraced his own life style.

Chapter Ten

"Utopia: Fishing the Keys"

"The Emergence of Bonefish Bob"
with Stephen F. Blanche as Proxy

A quiet March afternoon afforded Bob an early departure from the shop. Greg Thieman and Chet Pryor were assigned the crow's nest at Bonefish Bob's as lookouts for customers. Bob and his yellow kayak were on their way to the ocean at a little bay that stretched eastward to the open sea. He had a spin cast rod and reel set up and some live shrimp. On a whim, he also placed a Thomas and Thomas twelve weight in the hold of the small craft. A few hand-tied flies were attached to his vest.

From Anne's Beach near Islamorada, he had slid into the still saltwater of a cove that was protected from the steady, but mild, breezes of the day. Out from the shoreline about five hundred yards, he tied-off the kayak with a tether and a gnarled piece of driftwood which he carried for that expressed purpose. He had grown attached to the weather-beaten wood staff. Bob prized it for his tie-off when it emerged from the ocean. As a companion, it was tested and worn but sturdy and functional.

Bob's sliding, practiced walk to approach feeding fish was hard earned over many a winter fishing excursion, and he took pride in nearing the feeding "Bones" without spooking any of the school. "No tails, this afternoon," he muttered to himself, disappointed that it foretold of an evening that might not produce the electrifying take and run to which he had become addicted. He wondered what surprises lurked in the afternoon. He plodded along the flat noticing the tide rising into the cove. "Should be fish coming in on this rising water," he calculated aloud. Another fifty yards from his kayak, he rested surveying the lapping water. Still he sighted no tailing fish. He returned to the vessel, stowed the spinning outfit and bait and boarded.

Bob paddled to a cut between two mangrove islets in the distance. A darker pool of water lay on the southern point of the mangroves to his left. On foot again, he followed the sandy bottom sixty yards along the mangrove line. Resting, he surmised that the sun was a little too high, and the feeding fish were yet to come into this bay.

"Swoosh!" alerted him to a surfacing fish behind him and in the deeper pool. *Tarpon sucking air!* he reflected. It energized his senses when he read the map of nature and understood it. Guiding early in the mornings and sometimes late at night, he had often located tarpon by this sound. If his clients favored redfish or snook in their "bucket list", but were fortunate to hook up with a tarpon, it would make their day . . . and his. He checked his rod. One of his primary tenets, *Rod Tip Awareness*, shot into his consciousness. That was the term with which he christened this tactic of keeping the last ferrule always uppermost in one's mind. "This little spinning combo's not going to handle one of them," he muttered to the soft salt air. Excitement prompted his on-going soliloquy. "Not stout enough for a big tarpon." Already the kernel of a change of plan was working in his mind. It was the twelve-weight that he brought for tarpon.

Patiently, he retraced his sliding gate to the moored kayak and assembled the Thomas and Thomas. He set it up with his Islander LX4.8 reel. The large arbor reel held ample line. It was rigged with a fifty-pound shock leader to which he tied one of his favorite tarpon patterns. "What the heck! Why not give it a try?" he coaxed himself. It was five-thirty by the time he had double checked his knots and terminal gear. If he hooked into a juvenile tarpon with his set up, it would be a great day. The casts would be made from a seated position in his kayak. That he calculated would minimize the chance of a quick break-off of the fish. The frictionless contact of kayak and water would assist the bend of the rod and the drag of the reel.

He paddled the craft to a spot on the flat that permitted a drift toward the pool. The current then put him at a comfortable forty yards from the drop-off of deeper water. The mangroves nudged along the darker water. He speculated that a larger hooked fish would avoid the tangle of mangroves in favor of the open bay. The water rippled and churned all along the expanse of the pool. Bob knew now that it held more than one fish, for a sizeable school clouded the water with milky sediment. He could not spot fish, pick out one tarpon to take. This catch would be the "luck of the draw". False casts presented no problem as the coloration of the water prevented prey from seeing predator.

His shock tippet would give weight to the fly and increase the likelihood that the imitation bait fish pattern would descend into the feeding area. His own confidence buoyed his calm—he knew that anxiety and the rush of excitement were his enemies. The second false cast put his fly at the front edge of the pool. He wanted the whisper of a slap upon the water. With bonefish he placed his fly delicately, soundlessly on the surface; but, in the turbulence and feeding of these fish, sound was his ally. He counted to six, watching his line, fingering it with gentle pressure, and waited. Nothing nudged the fly, but the activity continued before him in the pool. He took up the slack on the water, lifted the rod tip and pulled the fly smoothly from the water into a back cast. In one continuous, fluid motion, he set the fly farther into the swirling pool. Again he waited patiently but primed.

The subtle curves and arcs that made up the slack line on the water ahead of him stretched and straightened almost imperceptibly like the arms of an awakening sleeper. He waited. "Not much line tension on my fingers," he deliberately spoke to himself, but he flexed his shoulders unconsciously. He waited for a tell-tale rush or flash of line movement, none of which occurred. *Some debris might have run along the line to the fly*, he surmised in quiet thought. When fishing, many duties are required as routine—clearing debris from the terminal end and keeping the fly natural and pristine. These can be the gristle on which success depends. But fishing is the surprise, the unexpected, and Bob understood and coveted this aspect of his art.

He elected to back cast again and, if the line was fouled, clear it and recast. Elevating the rod tip, he began the smooth lift that would draw the fly to the surface and into a back cast. The rod bent and held its position, focused on the point where line met water. He detected no pulsation, no throb and no run. "Snagged!" he blurted into the belly of the kayak with his head bowed down in disappointment. He had dropped the feathered line from his left hand and placed his palm on the gunwale. The right arm firmly gripped the stubbornly frozen rod, and his right fingers anchored the stretched line against the rod butt. He felt the kayak sway with his left hand, and his head popped up in an attempt to confirm what he had sensed. The line and the boat were swinging eastward matching a movement in the pool. "That's a fish, a big one!" he shouted to the bay. Stimuli raced across his consciousness. The size of the fish, the limits of the gear, the time of day, the equipment he brought, and the future were all on his mind.

Not yet aware of its dilemma, the fish stayed within the pool and merely tested the feeling of pressure in its mouth. The rod pulsed now with the repetitive chomping of lower jaw on fixed upper plate. The fish sensed a weight, a harness of some sort on its freedom. Others in the school read the bewilderment, and some rushed out of the pool in fear of some unknown message from the hooked fish. Another group dove into the depths of the murky, milk-stained waters. As if merely bothered by some inconvenience, the prey rolled and pitched onto the shallower water of the flat.

Bonefish Bob lost his breath with the vision of the monster tarpon which suddenly appeared at the edge of the turmoil. At first he was not certain that this was his fish, but its slow exit to the open ocean drew the kayak and rod tip irrevocably eastward. "Holy crap!" fell dangerously from his lips. Excitement, disbelief, fear and peril were painted into that lone exclamation. A rapid set of scenarios filtered through his thought process. How far would he go to land this fish? What was he willing to risk in time, tackle and life in this play which had just commenced? He determined to stick to a very strict plan. The slow, powerful tug from the pumping tail of the great tarpon towed the kayak and Bonefish Bob as effortlessly as a sled is pulled across a frozen pond. Within the first forty yards of his travels with this huge fish, Bob decided not to cut the line but to attempt to retrieve his fly from the mouth of the tarpon. That was his concession to landing the fish. Secondly, he determined to avoid breaking the rod tip. He knew the older rod would be irreplaceable, and this became an issue of pride for him. The kayak slid quickly in response to the fleeing tarpon each time Bob put any extra pressure on the rod and reel. He knew that his terminal line and gear would hold this fish as long as he did not anchor or create too much resistance to its runs. Lastly, this would be a legal catch if he could touch the leader and then release the fish. But could he reclaim his fly? This question dissolved in his mind as the fish, now tired of the stubborn barb in its mouth, attacked the fly and its tether.

Angry, the behemoth stormed into aggressive counter measures to tear the annoyance from its enormous sliver edged maw. In the shallow salt flats, the beast managed to lift its head and flail the surface in a maddened tirade intended to throw the hook. As it thrashed, it surged with unnatural power and fury, driving Bob and his kayak at precarious speed over the flats. Bob gathered all of his wiles about angling and big fish. The fisherman managed to give line as the forceful run ensued. The boat kept pace but separated itself from the fight gradually as more line was fed off the reel. It did not matter that he was alone; this was a private matter between man and the nature of the animal. The outcome was shrouded in uncertainty, dependent only on the endurance of this trophy tarpon and Bob's trusted gear.

The fight took on a ballet of its own: Bob gave up line to the reel's backing and then held on, allowing the kayak to trail the fish like a little brother following his older sibling to the corner store. The water deepened as the pair traversed vast distances. The two mangrove isles now sat a half mile from the fight. Bob realized that the fish had towed him beyond his put-in location along the cove. Getting back to his truck was not one of his concerns.

Suddenly, the line swung ocean-ward violently and Bob knew the tarpon was preparing to jump. The line surged upward like a crystal blue blade, exploding in white foam as it ripped through the blue sea. The monster broke into the air amid a plume of salt mist. It shook its head violently left and right trying to free itself of the foreign matter in its mouth. The full dimension of the fish was now presented to Bob in clear view against an early evening sky. "Good, Lord!" prayed Bob in an exclamation that humbled him. "I could put my head and one shoulder into its mouth!" A thunderous explosion of water burst into the air as the fish plunged into the bay. Driven by its failure, the tarpon veered southward beyond the bay and toward a cut that led into the Gulf from the Atlantic. Bob gave the fish its lead and journeyed with it out of the bay and into the cut.

The bridge over U. S. Route One came into focus a few hundred yards ahead. Bob saw the overhead traffic moving north and south, and his attachment to the tarpon lasted long enough to permit some distraction to enter the contest. There was some foot traffic also. As if drawn by magnets, the few walkers spotted the man in the yellow kayak and the tarpon on a leash. One teen was more animated than the others as he jumped, pointed, and gyrated with arms pointing down onto the stage of the fight. Three companions joined him to watch the spectacle as Bob and his fish passed beneath the bridge and headed to the gulf side of the waterway.

On the other side, Bob heard the calls from the youth who had traversed the road to watch the fisherman's progress. "Hey! Mister! You need any help?"

Bob sensed the futility of any assistance from the lad, but managed a wave overhead and back to the fellow. Then, as if understanding it had made a mistake, the tarpon turned, perhaps recognizing the confinement caused by the banks of the cut. Bob scrambled to bring in the excess line caused by the fish doubling back under him in its efforts to return to the Atlantic. Some of the tether went onto the reel, but the rest he lapped over the shell of the kayak. Back under the bridge the twosome danced. Their audience had grown to five people by the time Bob cleared the underside of the structure. He purged a pang of annoyance from the moment, for the audience had interrupted this private ritual.

"That's Bonefish Bob down there!" one of the spectators screamed in recognition of the fisherman and the infamous yellow kayak. Embarrassment was a luxury at that moment; the work at hand was to feed out the line that he had brought to the reel and onto the skin of the boat. With the speed of the giant, he had no time to crank the line to reel so it lay limp on the top of his skiff and draped loosely onto the water surface. Cautiously, he released all the line into the sea, minding especially the unfurling. A knot or a loop draped over a paddle or a rope would end the fight or even capsize the kayak. The line played out cleanly and the struggle continued.

The tarpon headed south again swimming toward Indian Key State Park. Bob was alone again with his struggle and it satisfied him immeasurably. His right arm ached from the unrelenting pressure applied by the giant, but he rested it by switching the pole to his rested left arm. The pace, ebb, and flow were steady, and their predictability afforded him a chance to glimpse at his watch. Time was inching toward sunset. Bonefish Bob calculated the time needed to paddle to his start-out point and accepted a landing after nightfall. The great fish could not be landed, of this he was sure. He added criteria to his original three-pronged plan. He would play the tarpon to the kayak. With no intention of cutting his line, he determined to fight the fish to the side of his boat and attempt to free the fly from its jaw.

Slowly the process evolved. Bob brought in line and simultaneously drew himself closer to his prey. The fish seemed unaware of the gradually diminishing distance which separated the combatants. The tarpon was indifferent to Bob's plan; its size dictated a sense of certain mastery over anything which entered its domain. The approach of the angler drew little heed from the creature. Bob pumped line onto the kayak and reeled twenty yards onto his spool. He wanted the luxury of a little play in the line, but too much slack would give the fish the upper hand.

Swimming arrogantly with Bob in tow, the tarpon had been eased calmly and securely to within ten yards of the yellow hull. One huge eye surveyed the boat as if it were an alien companion forced into an unwelcomed friendship. The eye spoke of concern and curiosity now, and Bob anticipated a flash of turmoil and flight from the animal. It never came. "Maybe, you're more tired than I thought," pondered Bob.

Almost spiritually, the great fish eased alongside the frail kayak. Bob felt a reverence seep into his being as he gauged the monster's length against the kayak. "He's eight foot at least," whispered Bob to the darkening salt air. "Got to weigh well over two hundred pounds," he calculated with homage and awe. He was linked by fragile line and leader to a wondrous animal. A sharp instinct shot through his being: this was a dangerous moment!

Adroitly, he reached into the kayak and felt the driftwood staff. The bait fish patterned fly was embedded in the lower lip of the tarpon, but it protruded forward due to the structure of the mouth. Bob held the rod high in his right arm with the line pinched firmly between his index finger and the butt. Several yards of line lay limp on the top of the kayak, ready for any run or roll by the fish. He chose the staff of driftwood to disengage the fly rather than the smooth scooped flange of his paddle. The driftwood was a natural object and not some foreign body thrusting its presence into the visceral drama. The tarpon rhythmically swayed left and right as it lulled next to the companion kayak. Bob had one chance to dislodge the fly, for he knew the giant animal would lunge and retreat from any probe that neared its mouth. Bob rested a notch at the bottom of the staff on the tippet just above the water surface—the fish did not seem to care. Deftly, he guided the wooden staff down the taut line by feel as he scanned the fish, seeking any movement that would signal its flight from the boat and the man. Two feet from the fly, the wood tip touched the ocean. Bob thrust the probe downward, sliding toward the hook end of the fish imitation. Simultaneously, the staff struck the fly and the mouth of the great fish. Explosively, the tarpon dove with lure still attached into the deeper water beneath the kayak. The craft heaved viciously downward and pivoted to the right, chasing ferociously after the retreating monster. Bob leaned hard left holding the rod in his right hand high above his head. The driftwood staff in his left arm waved backward and left, parallel to the sea for balance. He failed to dislodge the fly, and the testament to his attempt was a locomotive driven rush of speed and spray. The only good result Bob could imagine was that he still had the fish and his tackle.

Quickly, a second bridge rose before the southern run of the tarpon. Its position confirmed to Bob the distance that separated him from his drop-off point. He was quite far from his truck. Bob decided to make a last stand at that point, close to the shoreline, if possible, for safety. He used the time of the approach to secure his gear in the bowel of the kayak. When he was sure that all items were stowed, he gathered the tether line in his left hand and worked it into a loose loop. At the exit side of the bridge, his vision picked up a dancing ball of white. A channel marker was anchored just beyond the bridge decking. The tarpon angled to the right and away from the buoy. Bonefish Bob stretched backward and lay to his left, releasing line gradually from his reel. He produced a swing that projected his boat like a skier digging on his edges to complete a left hand turn. He tried to overrun the white target so that any chance of a miss would be minimized. For these fleeting seconds, the fish was the farthest thing from Bob's mind. He had to snag the buoy.

The front of the yellow craft struck the marker, and it slid along the length until it was at Bob's left hand. He only had to lay the loop over the ball, connect his rope to the buoy's underwater tether and secure the kayak to the marker. Cool and calculating, with only his reflexes to guide him, Bob accomplished the feat with little difficulty. He was pleased with himself until the full force and surge of the massive tarpon slammed into his rod and right arm. "Whoa!" he gasped, fearing the power that he was now sensing. Unseen, but fully known, it strove against him, deep within the ocean twenty yards from him.

The memory that he touched the leader when the first release failed gratified him—the tarpon was his. Now retrieving the fly was paramount. Bob could pry the fly from the fish by using the anchorage as leverage. His hope was to regain his fly, set the fish free, and not break his rod. The kayak fretted in the water, trying to follow the fish but repeatedly yanked backward by the buoy.

It rocked and cavorted like a thoroughbred anxious to break into the race. There was enough tension to free the fly, break the rod, or snap the line. Bob had no clear sense of what might happen.

A long shadow brushed onto the settled sea beneath the bridge. The giant tarpon shoved its huge head out of the water and twisted its head backward, scowling at the would-be captor. Its wet, silver tail spray dampened the early evening, and the back of the fish caressed the foam of the ocean in another descent into the depths. All went quiet as the fish took no line in its drop into the deeper water. Bob seized the line firmly in his left hand and aimed the rod horizontally at the last position of the tarpon. Now, Bob wanted to take control before the fish swam more line from his reel. Allowing the rod to run freely up and down the taut line, he yanked hard with both hands. His first unimpeded contact with the power of his adversary left him impressed. "You are one strong son-of-a-bitch!" he muttered in the direction of his singing line. Nothing gave: line, hook, fish, and kayak remained the same. He shimmied forward in the boat as much as he could and gathered more line that exited the ferrule nearest the reel. Thrusting his body backward toward the buoy, he pulled feverishly, tugging repeatedly on the entwined line. The securing grip began to cut into his hand. At the last violent pull, there was a snap and the surprising release. Then line recoiled onto itself at bullet speed. Bob heard the crack of impact of line on rod. As a frightened child seeks the embrace of its comforting parent, the rod leaped into Bob's right hand.

Hope shifted into neutral for Bob, for he recognized the "snap". There would have been less pop from a freed fly. A faint hint of possible success remained with him as he feverishly drew in the line from the water. The fish was gone but had it left him the prize? The tippet came onboard, but disappointment etched Bob's face. The fly was still with the tarpon. The animal had selfishly kept the bounty. Then the fisherman noticed in the glint of reflected light the ferrule at the tip of his rod dangling uselessly on the line with four inches of rod tip still attached. "Damn it! Damn It!" he shouted. He rested, stretched, but finally smiled into the onset of darkness.

Numbness took over as he began the routine of stowing and preparing for his run back to the truck and Islamorada. Unhitched from the buoy and with paddle in hand, he pivoted northward under the bridge and started home. Nine strokes into his voyage, giddiness overtook him. Adrenaline and joy, fatigue and elation, and solitude and nature blended into a perfection he had never sensed. "Whoa! Yeah! That was amazing! That was something else!" his voice celebrated as he glided homeward with continual pulls on his paddle. The effort of driving the blade just beneath the surface of the darkening blue water was exhilarating. Bob remained comrade to the kayak and to the night. The fatigue, the aching muscles and the darkness were enjoyed and coveted. "No money could buy this!" he reflected.

The next morning, a picture of a two hundred pound tarpon in the embrace of some stranger and his guide was posted on the customer side of Bob's cash register. Dangling from a punched hole in its upper right hand corner was the ferrule and tip of Bob's twelve-weight antique rod. Beneath the photo was a shot of Bob sitting in his big yellow kayak. What a story Bob was to tell! All day long, he just had to connect the dots.

Chapter Eleven

"Hooking Up With Aunt Tilley"

As told in part by Arthur Berger

In those years, Bob grew a rustic persona. Along with his recognizably small stature, he took pride in his unshaven, bearded face. He liked playing the part of an old salt. The beard aged into a salt and pepper bush of five or six inches and then transformed into a whiter snowy-like attachment. The gleam and sparkle of his sea-blue eyes became even more prominent aspects of his friendly appearance. A rumor in the Keys centered on legendary entertainer, Jimmy Buffett. Upon meeting Bob on one of several occasions, he described Bonefish as "Santa Claus with big feet."

The shop hours dictated Bob's available free time. With his lunch routine established, Bonefish Bob claimed to do his own fly fishing for bonefish, tarpon, redfish and snook later in the day or early in the morning when the winds were calmer. Many Floridians and northern friends had sightings of Bob tossing shrimp to bonefish and baitfish to tarpon. He never spoke of using live bait; but to all whom he met, his own storied legend painted him as the consummate fly fisherman. His Hewes sat idle in the water or on its trailer most times. He found his yellow kayak and the john boat more suitable to shallow water, to his time constraints, and to silently stalking his prey. The canoe-like craft was an ugly ten-foot-long hull that was easily recognized drifting atop the shimmering blue of the Atlantic or Gulf.

"I go out just about every day," related Bob to a customer as he marketed his guiding experience. "The fishing's been great. You can pretty much pick your fish. There are tarpon every-where. You can even pick the size you want." With a glimmer in his eye, he evaluated the Northerner on the other side of his counter. He reached down and tugged lovingly at the nape of his golden retriever, Devil. The dog spent as much time with Bob as possible. People were always amused to learn that the gentle hound was called "Devil". Even his dog had the mystique of the unexpected. "So, you're just picking up some odds and ends?" continued Bob.

"Yes, I have a free day tomorrow," responded the client. He was an athletic man in his fifties. Bob conjectured that he took good care of himself and could probably afford to do so. "I'd like to get on the water for a few hours." He looked up beyond Bob to a sign that publicized the guided trip rates.

With the man's line of sight passing overhead, Bob surmised that he wanted to do a charter. "Well, there are many good guides in Islamorada, but only a few great ones," he capitulated with a flick of his left shoulder in the direction of his rate poster.

"But I'm not ready to spend that kind of cash for four hours," he stammered.

"Well, you look around and, if you still don't find someone in your price range, come back; and I'll see what I can do," volunteered Bob. He figured the fellow wanted to negotiate a better price, but there was more fun in the customer doing some footwork.

With his wares in a brown paper bag, the gentleman from up north about faced and set his sails on the exit. Bob trailed after him. The man walked past his car, one of the few in the parking lot. He strode toward a fisherman tending his truck, trailer, and boat at the far northern side of the lot.

Jimmy Lopez was washing down the hull of his Carolina skiff. Florida registration numbers ran off the green hull. Jimmy sometimes guided for Bob, and they fished together many times. Bob surgically picked his brain as a matter of routine, but Jimmy felt that he had the better of the deal. He appreciated the fresh outlook that this Mainer gave to him regarding fly fishing. Jimmy had a resident's tan, one that separated "Year-rounders" from the seasonal visitors. His thick black hair was pulled tightly into a ponytail that accented his roundish face. He liked work, all kinds of work. Friends meant the world to him, and he was loyal beyond measure. He saw the tourist approach from the corner of his eye. *A tailing bone,* he imagined.

"Hi!" saluted the newcomer. "You do any guiding?" The stranger stood with the paper bag dangling in his hands behind his back and swayed to and fro.

"Yes, sir!" greeted Jimmy, aware that the man had just left Bonefish Bob's shop.

"How's the fishing?" continued the Northerner as he approached the hull of Jimmy's skiff.

"It's been pretty lousy lately," declared Jimmy, and then he added, "but tomorrow is another day."

"The fellow who runs the fly shop said the fishing's been great. Said he, 'goes out almost every day,'" a tint of confusion left his mouth with the report. *Two guides with two versions of the same story,* he mulled.

"Oh Bob, there!" reflected Jimmy, "that's his Hewes over there on the trailer facing the side alley." Jimmy drew the Northerner's attention toward the boat with a directing gesture of his right hand.

When the stranger turned and focused on the boat, he began to shake his head in low pendulum motions. "That boat hasn't seen open water in a long time," spoke the stranger.

The skiff sat idle but was securely fastened to the trailer. It was a Hewes, one he picked up after he gave up the Mitchell's Chris Craft. It had a single big Yamaha outboard attached. The white hull was trimmed in Bob's blue, and it sat in stark contrast to the dried green algae and slime that painted its underside. No recent lapping of tidal water had cleansed or removed the growth that resided under Bob's boat. A yellow kayak, attached aft of the boat, fidgeted loosely with the wind like a pet eager to take a walk with its master. Jimmy knew that Bob generally fished with his kayak and john boat. He sometimes took clients out on their own boats. Jimmy fondly remembered the youngsters from Montana and Maine using the Hewes in exchange for detailing the underside. Sometimes Bob sub-contracted his services to other guides and used their main skiff or their second boat to guide the customers.

"What's your going rate for one-half day, Captain?" The vision of Bob's boat sealed the deal.

The service was struck for fifty dollars less than Bob's posted rate, and the time and details were firm before the client left. Bob had the luxury of watching the unfolding of the deal, for no one arrived at the bait and fly shop during the proceedings.

The next morning, Chet Pryor was prepping Jimmy's boat for the half-day excursion. The client motored onto the lot and parked his vehicle as close to the skiff and as far from Bonefish Bob's shop as possible. The lot was empty save for Jimmy's rig, and the shop appeared to be closed. The customer emptied his car of two bags of gear, some rods, and a cooler. The figure of Greg Theiman appeared on the southern corner of the parking lot and ambled casually toward the shop. His shoes crunched the shells and gravel as he approached the front door. Shuffling with a set of keys, he opened Bonefish Bob's for business.

"You can bring that equipment with you, but you really don't need anything. Your guide will supply everything," explained Chet as the Northerner approached the boat. He leaned over the gunwale with a friendly hand extended and introduced himself, "I'm Chet Pryor and I'll be your mate today."

"Sure, pleased to meet you," cajoled the newcomer. "Where's Captain Jimmy?" petitioned the fisherman.

"He's out on the water already. He got an early morning call from a regular of his, but he set you up with the best guide in Islamorada. Jim took another boat," informed the diligent messenger who continued to set up the skiff and situate the client.

"Well, I guess, things like this happen?" muddled the fellow. "Who . . . where's the replacement?"

"He went out for some coffee and tea but he'll be right back," alerted Chet. The grinding of tires on seashells and the white dust from the loose fill of the parking lot signaled the arrival of a solitary truck from the highway. "That's him now!" pointed Chet.

Parking next to the Northerner's car, the guide shut down the engine, flung open the driver's side door and swung into the bright morning sun glare. With confident strides and carrying a cardboard tray of Styrofoam cups and sandwiches, Bob Berger sauntered over to the Jimmy Lopez Guide Service's boat and trailer. Devil pranced alongside his master.

The customer stood with mouth agape, arms at his side, and a million questions on his face. "Hey! What's going on here?" he mustered after a pause of several seconds.

Bob's right hand was extended and, with a smiling, friendly face, he approached the confused and suspicious fisherman. "Jimmy and I are partners, and we like to set up newcomers like this to . . . you know, relax them," confessed Bob with an air of harmlessness. He sent Devil back to wait at the shop or find his way home if he chose.

The group fished in the gulf and on the flats on the Atlantic side. Bob was right, for the catches were numerous and the fish were of good size. The client marveled at Bob's ability to spot fish in the chop. Sometimes, even without sunglasses or without an elongated brim on his hat, he would pick up subtle movements of fish in the currents and shadows and those tailing on bait.

During a lull in the action, Bob brought out sandwiches. The three set down the gear and picked up the conversation. Bob could not let the client go without hearing his favorite lobster story. With a spring in his step and a ham and turkey club in his hand, Bob gyrated about the flat deck of the skiff dramatically rendering the old Maine tale of Aunt Tilley.

"So this here lobster fisherman is visiting his Aunt Tilley one morning. She tells the nephew, 'I'd like to go out with you one day to get some lobsters.'" Bob delivered the line by playing the Aunt with a wonderful Mainer falsetto. Even though Chet had heard the story before, he still chuckled loudly. "Aunt Tilley, you have to know, is a large, very large lady; and her nephew is reluctant to take her out on the open seas. He promises with half a heart, 'I'll call you on a good calm day, okay, Aunt Tilley?' So he figures that's the end of that, until one day he gets a call from Aunt Tilley. 'Nephew, I found out that everyone in the family has been on that boat of yours except me. So you're taking me out for lobster tomorrow!' Well, the nephew was resolved to perform his requested duties, so he sets out with Aunt Tilley on one of his usual lobster pot retrievals."

The client and Chet ceased eating or drinking at this point and sat transfixed and mesmerized like school children at a circus. With the boat anchored in a quiet cove, only the lapping of gentle waves and an occasional scream from a gull interacted with the performance.

"All was going rather well. The nephew had just decked a pot full of lobsters when Aunt Tilley sprung from her mooring to get a close look at the contents of the pot. A rogue wave decided to slam the boat just as Aunt Tilley arrived at the pot. The wave lifted the boat and pitched it starboard leaving Aunt Tilley in mid air." Bob had stretched upward on tip toes to create the desired effect. His hand played the ballerina, putting Aunt Tilley in peril.

"Overboard she went," lamented Bob to his client and the captive mate. "Being so large, she went down like a lead stone." Bob paused to absorb the effects of his antics and gestures on the two men. "Yep, the poor nephew tried over and over again to snag her with his grappling hook, but he never hooked her. By law, he knew he had to contact the Harbor Master. So he gets on the CB radio and notifies the officials that he's lost Aunt Tilley overboard. The subsequent search party that combed the coordinates failed to turn up Aunt Tilley." Bob took a swallow of Sprite and a bite of club sandwich. The time wasted eating the morsel left the client in agony.

"Come on, Bob, what happened?" the customer had taken the bait, but Bob still taunted him with a slow consumption of vittles.

"A few weeks after the memorial service, the nephew is out collecting pots again, but he discovers one that is unusually difficult to bring on board. Low and behold, up comes the pot with Aunt Tilley in tow. As the nephew brings her aboard, he notices that there are two dozen or more lobsters clinging to her." Bob stopped and took a deep breath followed by a large draft of

Sprite. "Knowing his legal obligations, he calls the Harbor Master. 'Sir, I just pulled Aunt Tilley out of the ocean holding on to one of my lobster pots,' he reported, 'and she's stinking covered in lobsters. What should I do?' he says. There's a pause on the other end. 'If it's like you say, and she's covered with lobsters, I'd harvest all those lobsters and throw her back!'"

Of the three, Bob laughed best at his favorite story. Chet hoped to hear it retold many times. The Northerner wanted the minute details completely stored in his synapses; he was determined to retell it with Bob's same bravado.

The Northerner was introduced to the "Trinity," the "Triple," and the "Slam." They boated numerous snook, two juvenile tarpon, one redfish, and too many barracuda; but a bonefish and a permit were not to be found. Bob honored him with the notification that he had taken the "Gulf Slam." Little pewter pins, fashioned in replicas of sport fish, were awarded the Northerner to wear on his hat as trophies of his day on the water with BFB and Chet Pryor. That afternoon once on firm ground, handshakes, hugs, and best wishes were shared. The Northerner became one of the regular clients.

Chapter Twelve

"Snake Creek Guiding Company"

As told in part by William Coite

Steve's Time Out Bar-B-Q advertised great ribs and seafood Florida-style. The single story, ranch-styled eatery sat on the east side of Route One. It was two strip malls south of Bonefish Bob's shop. Sometimes he and Jan met with Pat and Donna Cutrone there. They found that the Keys made them fast friends. Many of the Mainers who came south to fish and relax with Bob also made Steve's their watering hole. Chet, Jimmy, and Bonefish held counsel at the window table in the middle of the restaurant. Customers coming in the door at the lower end of the establishment had a clear view of the "locals" seated at Bob's table. Bill Coite, who was in town to do some tarpon fishing with Bob and Jimmy, came through the door with a splash of afternoon sunshine. His milky, sunscreen coated legs flashed white in his entrance.

"I didn't think I'd need to put on my Ray-O-Bans in here," taunted Jimmy. His bright smile mocked the pale skin of the freshly arrived Mainer.

"Hey, don't you put down these legs. They get me through some pretty tough Maine winters. You guys have it soft," retaliated Bill in self-defense.

Chet, who was seated between Bob and Jimmy, leaned forward on his elbows and made a feeble effort to stand. He craned his head over the table and directed his eyes downward toward Bill's feet. "Those are pretty handsome winter road markers you got there."

"Great! You're the one guy I thought who'd leave me alone, Chet," pleaded Bill. He pulled out the vacant chair that was tucked under the tabletop. It slid into the passing lane of any traffic headed to the restrooms. He felt immediately like a witness about to be grilled by the judge and two attorneys.

"I'll always stand by you," chimed Bob, "even though you come down here and wear out my equipment." The comment flicked into the reunion like an adolescent snapping the earlobe of a friend who just arrived.

In feigned disinterest, Bill picked up a menu. But then, with a pout that expressed injured feelings, Bill countered, "What? That Q-Mart Special fishing gear and used stuff you sell down here!" Jimmy liked that comment too much, and it brought a nudge from Bob's left forearm.

"My collectors' items, the Winstons and the Thomas and Thomases serve my clientele very well, thank you, Mr. Coite," emphasized Bob.

"Oh! Watch out Bill, he's using the 'Mister' stuff!" warned Jimmy now taking Bill's side.

"Yeah, Bob, what about the broken rod tip you have at the register! That can't be good for business," countered Bill sensing he had a cohort in Jimmy.

Shaking his head like a fighting tarpon, Chet warned, "Don't go there! That's the trophy. That's like the sacred cow, the story-to-end-all-stories." Chet's reverence effectively ended the banter.

The meal came and the afternoon details were prepared in full. Two boats would go out—Chet and Bob in one; and Bill and his guide, Jimmy, in the second skiff. Earlier in the week, Jimmy had spotted tarpon along Snake Creek. The group marked a stretch along the old train line which years ago ran down to Key West during the twenties. Foraging fish schooled along several breaks near the railroad line. At intervals, some of the original structures were still visible above the surface of the gulf water, and it was good fishing water.

Bob checked in with Greg Thieman at the shop before he went to join the group at the ramp. Greg had a rough afternoon the day before. Bonefish Bob was tough on him when Greg's drinking got the better of him. Bob had sent him home with a stern warning to be back in good condition to run the shop the next morning or he would be finished at the shop. Greg knew he meant it. In many ways, Bob stabilized Greg's life, put him in good company and gave order to his life. This morning, Greg was fresh and anxious to put in a full day for Bob. The man was grateful and, as a result, grew into a trusted and loyal associate of Bob's.

From the ramp, a bounding, thrashing race ensued through the flat bay westward to the satellite marking. The skiffs and crews faced salt spray and endured bottom pounding waves during the twenty minute scamper to the fishing site. Jimmy eased his boat into a calmer trolling speed as his longitude and latitude mark came up on the guidance system. Chet followed in his wake, keeping a forty yard distance from the other team. When Jimmy powered down, so did Chet. Bob was busily rigging his own gear for tarpon. Jimmy had spent the earlier preparation time on shore setting Bill's two eleven-weight rods and large spool reels. Bob trusted Jimmy to decide on the terminal tackle and flies.

Bonefish prepared two rods: one held a two inch crab imitation and the other was tipped with a sparkling six inch streamer with chartreuse and white plastic filaments. Both baits glittered with reflective metallic flecks imbedded in the materials. Bob had no idea what Jimmy tied to Bill's gear, but he hoped that they were significantly different from his selections. The more varied the lures, the better chance of finding out what the tarpon were taking.

Chet's lean frame eased into the twenty-one foot graphite poling lance at the rear of Bob's Hewes, and the flats boat slid smoothly along the shallows. The surface toward Snake Creek was dotted with a small cluster of mangroves and decaying trestles from the old railroad. Bob and Chet decided to man the poling chores alternately as fish were hooked, but Jimmy had the full duty on board his skiff. Bill, as guest, was spared the labor of the hunt. Being friends did not forego a sizeable tip to Jimmy if the day went well.

A low whistle from Bob perked Jimmy's ears, and he immediately scanned the surface in the fishing area. He did not look to Bob for he knew the signal meant fish were sighted. The two skiffs glided silently quite a distance apart. Nearer to Jimmy, Chet eyed the tell-tale wakes from fish rolling on bait. He read the convoluted roll of the water; there were no long darting lines, but rather white chalk oozed from beneath the movement.

"Ten o'clock," whispered Jimmy to his anxious Mainer. Bill stood on the flat forward deck ahead of the center console. He pivoted from a two o'clock perspective to the ordinance point given by his captain. "Get out twenty-five yards of line! Keep it smooth on the deck," he commanded softly with calm deliberation. No hurry or trepidation marked the guide as he tried to instill in his fisherman the need for composure.

Bob stood with Chet as silent witnesses to the hunt. The courtesy was to allow the visitor the first cast and hopefully the first hook-up. Bill shuffled his feet, causing the boat to pitch left to right. Bonefish Bob grimaced, biting his tongue rather than call out to his northern friend.

"Be still," petitioned Jimmy. "Don't want to spook any now." The visitor glanced backward with a thousand questions on his face. "Look, Bill, one false cast and try to get about twenty yards out. No problem!" he coached.

Rod tip slanted upward. "Bob," raised Chet, "he's throwing an all white caribou, the one with the big bug-eyes." The forward cast was on its way in an infinity-shaped, figure eight loop.

"He might get away with that one," mumbled Bob. Pursed, flattened lips bit more criticism at his friend than did his comment to Chet.

The guide was summoning all the skill and practice he could for his student. "Hold onto that! Don't move it yet," he instructed. "If you get a strike set the hook sideways, parallel to the surface. Don't raise your rod tip!" The party had discussed the unusual shape of the tarpon's mouth and how the strike drew the hook forward to the upper jaw. "Start stripping in the line . . . short, slow burst," came as the directive.

Bill eyed the water with the scrutiny of a laboratory researcher. He heard the voice and watched the water. Nothing else entered his conscious state. But uncertainty, his enemy at the moment, surfaced. His doubt erased the small glimmers of confidence he had garnered while following Jimmy's instructions. He began to pull in the fly with an accelerated tempo.

"No, no!" coaxed Jimmy into the back of the Mainer, "you got a chaser there. Slow it down!" Suddenly, a large swell of water engulfed the end of his line, but Bill only guessed at the position of his fly. He never saw the fly or the fish. The fly rested alone in the water.

"This isn't NASCAR, Bill!" flung Bob from his watchtower. He scaled the transom platform at the aft on his skiff and stood perched above the arena. He opted to wear sunglasses, especially above the water on the platform.

Jimmy manned the loftier position on the second boat. Once Bill missed the first fish, Jimmy made every effort to encourage the Mainer, "Not to worry, Bill! The tarpon are still there. You just popped the fly out of its strike zone." His encouragement spoke to the bowed head of the dejected fisherman. "Bob, you leave my client alone, ya hear!" badgered Jimmy with a false threat across the water to his business partner.

"Jimmy, you have no way of knowing how bad he treats me up at Nubble Light when we're on rockfish," philosophized Bob in his own defense.

"Let's get him one first, Bob" retorted Jimmy to the adjacent boat. In the front of the skiff, Bill had regained his focus and prepared to recast his line. "Let me pole us back a bit," he suggested. The delay allowed Bill to gather his wits and go mentally through his plan of attack. "More like eleven o'clock now, Bill, and about thirty yards," directed the guide.

A roll of the arm upward and the pull from the bending eleven-weight sent the fly backward in a smooth arch. Then, in a fluid retracing of its line, the fly darted into the target area. "Um!" drummed Bob with approval and a little more pride in his friend's abilities as a fly fisherman. Jimmy was silent this time.

"It's all his," announced Bob to Chet who nodded, acknowledging that he also noted the near-perfect cast.

The caribou ghost with beady eyes sailor-dove headfirst into the gulf with a "plunk". It descended into the school. Bill had no idea of how many tarpon picked up the flitter of white tail undulating in the white silt of the gulf. The body of the fly swam with fearless folly amid the fish in the pool. Then it was gone. Bill had only the snap jerk sense of an electric shock in his left fingertips. Engorged, only a tidbit of its length driveled from the mouth of the tarpon. The line snapped taut and, in a fraction of a heartbeat, Jimmy advised, "Sideways set, Bill, sideways set!" The game was on!

The five-footer stretched upward, moistening the afternoon between the boats with a chaotic and drenching aerial assault. The spray of salt water from its maddened torso flailed at the heavens. The tarpon fought the air as if it were the villain which had ensnared it. Three, four, five jumps, and Jimmy and Bill stopped counting. Fear honed Bill's efforts, and he forced himself to employ his instincts and his learned responses with big fish. The power and speed were deftly analyzed and the tension calculated. Jimmy was pleased to see the man working the fish with such skill. Bill adjusted to the first frantic runs and now the equipment took over. Enjoyment played amid the conflict. He was in no hurry and that too gave pleasure to the guide. After five minutes of the fight, the fish and the skiff moved well beyond the original coordinates of the fray.

Bob and Chet dutifully waited through the onset of the contest. They watched the "take", the set, the runs, and the battle as it settled into a stand-off. "See if you can hook up in there, Chet," encouraged Bob. "That fish is out of the pool and he may not have spooked the others." Chet almost succumbed to the temptation, but opted to share Bill's moments with his first tarpon. Ten minutes passed.

"Neither of them seems tired, Chet," evaluated Bob as he now leaned uselessly on the pole, holding ground on the spot of the first strike. Chet gave him a "Yes, I know" bob of his head and spat into the gulf.

Fifteen minutes elapsed and the jumps were less frequent and runs were shorter. The tarpon turned back as if searching for companions in his time of need. "He's tiring, Bill," prompted Jimmy. "You'll have him boat-side soon."

"Yeah, you'd better get that puny little critter to the boat before you hurt yourself!" challenged Bob. Chet was laughing aloud, satisfied that Bob prompted some action to quicken the landing process.

"We don't want to still be here tomorrow! Boat the darn thing!" added the now courageous Chet.

"Quiet you two! Leave the guy play out his fish!" shouted Jimmy, now peeved by his companions in the other boat. He knew Bob was not serious about any of his comments, but Chet was another question. He did not wish for Bill's moment in the sun to be clouded by guys who could fish for tarpon every day. The earnestness and forcefulness in his voice sat Chet down, laying his rod and reel on the deck. Chet conceded to the request and realized his position in the party.

Twenty minutes into the fight and the tarpon was no longer green. It lulled beside the skiff, quiet enough for Jimmy to secure it with both hands, grabbing the lower jaw. Bill put down his rod, grabbed his Pentax, and exchanged his package with Jimmy's. The orchestration was unpracticed, but the dance went perfectly. Bill secured the tarpon, Jimmy had the camera, and the necessary photos were snapped. Camera out of hand, Jimmy twisted the fly from the fish using his needle-nosed pliers. The souvenir was safely on board. A gentle but heavy swoosh sent the giant back into the gulf. The Carolina skiff bobbed up and down with each succeeding leap from Bill. Jimmy joined Bill with back slapping congratulations.

"Way to go, My Man!" screamed Bob in celebration and, as an after though, he added, "Cut the dancing or you'll scare the rest of the fish!"

Bob and Chet fished undisturbed for many minutes as Bill merely sat quietly evaluating himself and his energies. He needed down time, and Jimmy passed a cold bottle of beer and a small bag of pretzels to him. They hardly spoke for the true conversation had already taken place. The day was made. The other tarpon that were landed or lost that afternoon took second place to the pivotal battle between Bill Coite and his tarpon.

The boats returned to the ramp behind Bonefish Bob's shop and Jimmy Lopez's Guide Service. Their work was finished for the day. No one hurried to clean up or to stow gear. For the sake of rehydration, a few cold ales were divvied out. Devil made a brief appearance, nudging his muzzle on Bob's salty knee. He then sauntered into the shadows of the stoop in front of the shop.

An hour passed full of praise, old memories and good natured practical jokes. When Bob began to swing the three foot gaff like a nine iron, it signaled the terminus of the camaraderie. Chet stowed the gaff in its clamps beside the live-bait well, and Bob began his now traditional "Hug Fest". He paraded by the edge of the water at the bottom of the ramp. Jimmy and Chet entered into the custom easily as Bob had endeared them to the process. It was by now second nature to his friends in the Keys, but Bill had forgotten the ritual. He was caught in the role of a groundling, first watching the actors from afar, and then suddenly called upon to join them on stage. His ruddy-tinged, tan faced friend from Florida closed in on him from a few paces away. Bill suddenly sensed what was coming in the form of the beguiling, elfin fisherman. Bob's tenacious grasp smothered Bill, almost upended him. The twosome was an awkward one, and Bob's refusal to disconnect steered them backward. Bob's low moving frame drove them off the end of the ramp. Shallow, warm water awaited them with the greeting of a tumultuous splash. There stood the two Mainers, knee-deep in the gulf, still in Bob's affable embrace. Even the neighbors heard the roar of laughter from the four men which ended their day with Jimmy Lopez's Guide Service.

Chapter Thirteen

"Cabins and Sewing Baskets"

As told in part by David Sowerby,
William Mitchell, and Jan Wood

By 1992, Bob initiated the tradition of leaving the Keys each off-season with Jan. Religiously, for at least two weeks, the couple traveled to Ennis, Montana. Their return to the Keys became a flexible event, but Bob generally returned by the late summer. All was right with the world. He spent time with the family, traveled widely and savored his choices.

The spry, independent woman, Jan Wood, became Bob's endearing companion. Their shared time took them from York to Islamorada and to Ennis. The couple added the third stop to their annual migration, and the triangle was complete. Their 1995 trip to the Northwest, however, proved most eventful.

Lunch at "The Reel Decoy" in downtown Ennis evoked a nostalgic blend of rustic cowboy lore, hunting memorabilia and fly fishing dreams. The walls, décor and customers abounded in Montana ambiance. Bob and Jan gravitated to its welcoming atmosphere as easily as to the York and Islamorada eateries that they regularly visited.

Bob and Jan took advantage of their trip into town to stop for lunch one afternoon. A matronly woman and a companion sat nearby having a light lunch. She was talkative and boisterous enough to attract some attention to her conversation. The companion was familiar to Bob, for he recognized her as Betty, the wife of one of the local ministers. The other vociferous woman appeared to be a sister or close kin to the local. "Yes, Betty, since Henry and I divorced, I have no desire to stay in Montana anymore," bemoaned the lady. Her salon-bought bluish hair was wrapped neatly above a rounded face. A rosy complexion accented her lustrous smile. The Midwesterner's delivery continued, "I'm putting the Ennis cabin up for sale."

With a subdued, conciliatory tone, the local hummed in agreement, "Sue, that's probably a very good idea for you at this time of your life." After a brief pause which permitted Bob to turn fully around and face their table, Betty added, "What are you thinking of asking for it?" She spotted the round elfin face of Bob Berger sighting in on them from his window table. Betty asked the question with a practical purpose. Attaching a monetary amount to the divorce might alleviate any lingering pangs of disdain still held by her companion toward the wayward Henry. But now, the minister's wife felt intruded upon, almost embarrassed by the third party's interest in their conversation. She sent a disciplining glance in Bob's direction, but he would have no part of that.

Bob rose onto his feet and excused himself, offering a non-verbal gesture to Jan.

The divorcee uttered unemotionally, "Oh, Betty, I would take twenty thousand just to be free of it."

Bob had only to hear "Ennis" and headed straight to the pair with no inhibitions. "Excuse me ladies, but I happened to hear about this cabin in Ennis . . ." he interjected as his only introduction. In the midst of completing his comment, he pulled up a chair and proceeded to seat himself between the women.

The woman, Sue, tried to ignore his presence and complete her thought to Betty, "I don't know where he got his obsession for Big Sky, but it must have been from those fly fishing magazines that he was always reading."

The man, present next to her, would not be ignored. ". . . and you say you want to sell it, Ma'am?" questioned Bob just as if she had never spoken. Somehow, he managed to arrive at their table without completely startling them. Bob's demure carriage, sparkling eyes, and friendliness subdued any apprehension that the pair may have felt. He remained at their table for quite some time.

Jan sat perplexed nearby, entertained by the show evolving before her. The volume of the voices descended into near secrecy. Jan tried to figure the trend of the conversation from the visual clues offered by the threesome. The tease of disinformation made her anxious to learn the gist of the proceedings as soon as possible. With her head buried in the menu, Jan waited patiently for any news that might relieve the mounting suspense.

A chair spoke up nearby with its guttural rubbing on the oak floor as Bob pushed himself away from their table. In two rakish, satisfied strides, Bob returned to Jan. His face beamed with pride at his own self-discovery. It was an honest display, not one intended for others to see. He was extremely pleased with whatever had transpired over the last few minutes.

"What was that all about?" breathed Jan calmly with a feigned nonchalance of disinterest. She did not have to wait long for the explanation, for it fell from Bob like extra apples in an already full basket.

"Oh, I just bought us a cabin here in Ennis for twenty thousand dollars!" beamed Bob.

"Are we able to afford it?" supplied Jan with a poise that even surprised her. "Weren't you considering expanding the business or buying another boat?"

Bob did not let that economic uncertainty spoil his moment of elation. "I just figure if somebody throws you bait that you can't refuse, you take it," he philosophized. "Besides, it's an investment in something we do together," he added in a devil-may-care tone. So there he pontificated, the proud owner of an unseen Montana cabin. "Any new boat will have to wait," he calculated. He smiled broadly for, as far as he was concerned, he was set for life. The debt he had accrued meant nothing to him.

Eventually, the couple summered for varying weeks in Montana and visited York to see their families and old friends. Jan took a longer residence there each year. Bob was lured by native trout on the Madison and Upper Missouri Rivers, but he usually stayed only a few weeks. He found solitude from his labors and his comrades. He did not have a love-hate relationship with people, but rather it was a fatigue-rest relationship. His associates through the fishing contacts, the earlier clients of his tire and auto business, and even friends sometimes impinged upon his being. The people surrounding Bonefish Bob exhausted him psychologically. At times, like cabin fever, he sensed some larger force almost foisting them upon him during the year. Although generous to a fault with his time, in Big Sky country he could be restive, invigorated, and monastic . . . almost religious. He refused to drink from a half empty glass.

* * *

Jan's brown tresses cascaded in straight lines which surrounded her roundish face. Her stature rested just a minnow's length above Bob, but they were equals. With a girlish hold on her freckles, she matured throughout the casual years in Islamorada. At first, the relationship flourished amid the local color of York and then the glamour of the Keys. Jan Wood had invested a goodly part of her life in Maine and attended the university there. Now she willingly became a catalyst for Bob's growth in Islamorada. She enjoyed dining out, but the rite, frequently, had obligations attached. Pragmatically, reservations and appointments often dealt with a job, a required meeting, or some scheduled date. The ease of their lifestyle, however, drew them closer together at their favorite haunts: Steve's Time Out Bar-B-Q, The Reel Decoy, Norma's Kitchen, Rick's Café, and then at the houses of mutual friends for cards and long chats. They filled the sultry evenings, winter afternoons, and summer mornings. Dr. H. C. Palmer and his wife, Valerie, and others enjoyed their company whenever and wherever their courses met.

No task left Jan in a quandary; she picked each one up like a carpenter lifting a tool belt. She liked the hands-on approach to life, even people. The Mainer in Bob was mesmerized by her outgoing, gregarious energy. Her constant activity kept her fit, and she wore her Keys' tan well.

When the little office attached to the back of Bob's shop went up for rent, she proved to be a bit of a risk-taker. Jan had done custom sewing for friends for years, and it was a hobby of sorts. The idea to start her own boutique came in a dream she had one night. At lunch one rainy day, she captivated Bonefish

Bob with her revelation of her newest venture. Bob ate politely, fluffed his beard, and sat politely attentive to her aspirations.

"So, I'm talking to you in the parking lot, *and* I look over your shoulder, *and* it's a still, hot night," she rambled with excitement that etched every "and". "*And* I see this flashing neon sign over the door of that little back room office, and it says, 'Keep You in Stitches'. The sign has a needle and thread in white and blue attached to the upper right hand corner." She savored a long breath and a sip of iced tea. The tumbler dripped moisture onto the table top and rained onto her lap. The condensation distracted Bob, but Jan continued with accelerating interest and excitement. "Then I leave you there and walk in. People greet me. Pat and Donna are there and so are Dr. Palmer and Valerie. Customers are buying odds and ends. Some are at this long counter with clothes they've brought to have altered. It's amazing, Bob. I've already spoken to the rental agency this morning about that room behind your shop."

A quick bite of her BLT required Bob to make a comment. "Sounds like you're moving ahead with this, Jan," summarized Bob, still not exactly sure what he was supposed to say. The quizzical look that accompanied his words pried a commitment from Jan.

"I'm going to open it," was her rhetorical confession, "next month!" The last two words were shot like canon fire into the dining room.

A myriad of answers from Bob were delivered without words. He shuffled on his seat, scratched the back of his head, nodded in total agreement and sat back.

"You'll enjoy having me as your back door neighbor, Bob," she informed him. He broke out in a smile, broad enough to be easily seen behind the growth of beard that sometimes concealed his truer intentions.

"I know that when you have your mind set on something, Jan, it usually moves ahead like a bonefish tailing for shrimp. You don't miss anything." As he spoke, he simultaneously accepted the idea that Jan's new business would be sharing his parking lot. He did not mind it one bit.

Over the weeks prior to the grand opening, Jan was busy renovating the space. Even though Bob volunteered his services, she notified him that everything was under control. She tackled some flooring, patched a few of the walls, constructed functional counters and shelves, and painted the walls. With her able carpentry work, Jan easily dispatched the preparatory chores that left the "office" a comfortable shop space.

With the two businesses in operation, their lives became more intensely shared. They arrived together in the mornings, and many days the shops closed together. The people in their individual lives and their shared life became interwoven. The two business ventures smoothly incorporated their associates, friends and families. Together they hosted and cherished their Maine friends, his children, the young guides from Montana and the people they knew in Ennis. He was adopted by her local friends, and Bob enjoyed the time spent with her family when they visited.

Darker moods sometimes crept into the smooth seas, the balmy springs and the colorful falls of his days. Foreboding tempted his joy. Should life be this good to him? When is the storm going to hit? Jan sometimes sensed this quiet introspection in Bob. These were his private musings, and she knew he would share them when he was ready. However some, she surmised, were not within his power to reveal.

* * *

Late in April on a morning in 2001, bedazzled by ennui, three lads who had been wintering in Key Largo from Montana arrived at the doorstep of Bob's trailer. It represented itself as a stationary mobile home which rested on cinder blocks above a mangy plot of ground. The sand and shell lot was sparsely covered with stubbles of weeds, tufts of Bermuda grass, and a smattering of non-descript greenery. Some dwarf palms and a large Mimosa decorated the front lawn. A shell and gravel parking area abutted the western edge of the property. Bob's beloved sea blue trim, borrowed from the work done on the shop, laced the perimeter of the structure and succeeded in drawing some attention from the faded and tarnished siding. The home squatted in a northwestern suburb on a winding, one-lane blacktop road that snaked between the gulf and Route One. It sat a short walk from the shop. The three guides found him at home at 74 Lower Matecumbe Drive.

Kirk Gammill could have been the basketball player of the threesome as he towered above all of them. He hailed from Idaho but went to college in Northern California at Humboldt State University. He played collegiate soccer and honed his fly fishing skills on soccer trips and weekend breaks all over the West. On guided trips, bread baking was a specialty of his, and it landed him an interview in Rachelle Rae's magazine which featured guides who cook. He met Steve Blanche and Adam DeBruin at Humboldt.

Bonefish Bob and Kirk played cribbage religiously when the young man was in Islamorada. Bob once bragged that he had collected over fifteen hundred boards. As many times as the two played, a new board appeared to tally the lopsided score. The "Bonefish Board", an antique fifty year old board, and many others were the arenas of Bob's repeated whippings of his apprentice, Kirk. The one lucky victory that Kirk dealt to Bob caused such a reaction in the fiery gamer that Bob banned Kirk from his shop for three weeks.

Art Berger told everyone that his brother, Bob, "Should be a millionaire!" His theory was based on countless jobs, sales, requested work, and guided trips that Bob repeatedly turned down because of an on-going cribbage game. In York, he refused customer's requests for brake and engine work when he was in the midst of a contest. The fly shop saw similar refusals to befuddled customers during these serious competitions. Cribbage, not money, was his passion.

Adam was the Maine connection as he had grown up in York with Joe Sowerby. His claim to fame as a fisherman was the title he had garnered as a youth in Maine. Under the tutelage of local fly fishermen, he became the Fly Tying Champion of Maine. His bright blue eyes and Irish complexion were painted fair by his close-cropped red hair. It was curly when he allowed it to grow longer.

Steve was a transplant from Pennsylvania who spent some college years at Juniata College in the central part of the state. While playing soccer there, he fished the myriad of limestone streams that pock the famous fly fishing area of the state. His skills and interests flourished; and, when he transferred to Humboldt State University in California, soccer and fly fishing already agreed with him. He now resided in Key Largo in the winter months and in Missoula, Montana, during the summer trout fishing season. He was the middle man in stature among the others. It was Adam and Bob who saw eye to eye on mostly every topic, both literally and figuratively.

Bob was bare-chested and wielding a cup of hot tea when he answered the door. He eased into his mornings, but the fellows were comfortable with him during any part of the day. "Did you tie any of those patterns I showed you, Adam?" was his replacement for a morning greeting. The door swung inward and admitted the trio to the shadowy front room.

"Kirk, Steve and I tied up quite a few variations," responded Adam, pleased to report that he had done his homework.

Kirk handed a loosely filled plastic box to Bob. The mentor began to finger through the chaos of feathers, plastic filaments, hooks and plastic orbs, some with black beads that rattled when the fly was moved about. "Uh, I hope they catch you a mess of bones," was his appraisal.

That comment reminded Steve of Bob's opinion of the Pennsylvanian's first boat. Bob had looked over the aging hull of The Red Tide; and, so as not to disappoint the young first-time captain, simply tapped the boat confidently and said, "You'll catch a lot of bonefish with her."

"It seems to me you said something like that about my boat, Bob," added Steve. "But we're wondering if the flies will 'catch a mess of bones'," continued Steve, using Bob's own comment to present their motives to him. "Adam thought we might get a chance to go out with you," he invited.

"Got to open the shop this morning," mulled Bob, "'cause I got a guy coming in to pick up some gear he ordered." The boy in the man appeared saddened.

"Well, we don't expect to get out 'til later," prompted Kirk. "Adam said if we used your skiff, we'd have to clean her up anyway." No hint of any distance in their relationship entered his words. As fishermen, they were friends eons ago; some primal bond tore away any social awkwardness.

"Sure, you boys can take her out," permitted Bob, and then he added, "If my customer picks up his gear, I'd like to join you." As far as the friends were concerned, that was a deal sealed in stone. The foursome drove to Bonefish Bob's shop in Adam's crew cab. They would be Bonefish Bob's transportation home unless he decided to walk. They yearned to spend the day with him.

Jan had already opened his shop and hers. She met the truck in the lot. Wide awake and cheerful, she was pleased to see the young men delivering Bob. Devil pranced about, happy to see the young men with Bob. "Now what plans for the day have the four of you been contriving?" drilled Jan with a giggle that betrayed her feigned reproachful demeanor.

Kirk jumped to defend the group, "We're just taking Bob fishing!" he pled. Having spoken the unnecessary, he absorbed the jibes and pummeling of his companions for missing the obvious intent of Jan's comment.

The threesome readied and primed the Hewes for the afternoon of tracking bonefish. After two hours it leaned heavily on its moorings like the prizefighter bounding on the rope awaiting the opening bell. Chet approached the three friends with his eyes searching the ground just before each step. Adam sent a smirk back to his companions before vaulting from the deck to the ramp to greet Chet. Steve and Kirk knew the message's content before Chet spoke. "Bob's not going to join us," interpreted Steve to Kirk.

With repeated swings of his head, Kirk sent his agreement as feedback to Steve. Adam and Chet seemed to have little to

say, and they parted crisply with an air of determination that
sent Chet to his required chores and Adam to fishing with his
two friends.

By one o'clock, just before the incoming tide, the three were
under power and searching out bonefish. They headed straight
for Berger's Flat, as the captains in Islamorada were now call-
ing this bonefish haven. In the absence of Bonefish Bob, Adam
sat back and directed the whole operation through Kirk at the
console. Steve busied himself as mate, preparing gear and trying to spot schools of feeding fish. Finally, on Berger's Flat, they
scanned its deeper holes and the long shallow sands which abutted scattered mangrove islands. When the motor was killed, the
three took turns poling the craft to suspected hot spots.

It was just about this time of day that Robert Berger opened
the till of the register, removed an uncounted number of one
dollar bills, stuffed them into his back pocket, and exited the
front door of Bonefish Bob's Fly Shop. Chet sent his "Have a
good day!" shout after him, but it slammed into the swinging
door. Bob never heard him. Bob was on his way to Woody's, the
gentlemen's club up the strand from his shop. The dancing girls,
illuminated with confetti light, enchanted Bob in the darkened
barroom afternoon. His mood did not entertain fishing that day.

The trio, made up of a Pennsylvanian, a Mainer and an
Idahoan, could only imagine a day spent with Bonefish Bob. It
may have happened when a large school of bonefish gave Bob
its position with its knife-edged silver tails flailing in the pulsing rays of wave-scattered light. The day would be painted in a
dreamscape that they could only have imagined.

* * *

Steve propelled them silently to within a hundred yards
of the numerous glistening shards of silver triangles piercing
the water surface. Bonefish Bob would have watched as Steve
tied-off the nineteen foot poling rod which he had worked back
and forth until it was embedded securely in the coral and sand.
Bob would have observed each of the three pick out flies from

their treasure trove. Each took an assortment and pinned them to various holders on their persons: cap, wool strip, label, shirt sleeve. Each began the tedious, but well-trained, tying of the fly to tippet and leader. Each wet the pre-knot in the mouth, drew it to the mouth again, stretched it tight, and bit the extra filament from the end of the knot. And so it would have continued . . .

"No, no, no," stammered Bob, lifting himself heavily from his seat behind the console. The trio turned in unison to pay homage to the voice. He slithered around the central steerage and strode dramatically upon Adam as if he were stalking a deer on Ledge Mitchell's York property. "Lookie here!" he ordered of Adam. His arms were bent behind him, and he thrust his head forward, leading with his jaw. He presented to Adam a full face of teeth, which shown out from the fluff of his white beard. With his right hand, he now pointed to his mouth to accent the attention he wanted to place on his smile. Within six inches of Adam's face, he clarified, "You see these . . . these pearly whites?"

Adam nodded in affirmation; but, before he could say a word, Bob veered right, stalking Kirk. On his toes before the six foot four Idahoan, he put his left and right hands on either side of his mouth and gritted between his rabid smile, "These here . . . these here, Kirk!"

Another abrupt turn dismissed Kirk in mute bewilderment. Bob's agile stride quickly put him upon Steve who had coyly attempted to excuse himself from the demonstration. "Steve, you see these . . . these here teeth?" Steve bobbed his head like a ceramic puppy in the back window of an auto. "Let me see yours!" commanded the teacher. The young Pennsylvanian, at first unsure of exactly what was requested, managed to eke a minimal smile into the question on his face. "You've got a couple of rectangular slits in those teeth, Son" he posed.

Each was now rolling his tongue across and around his mouth, trying to detect the truth of Bob's observation. Steve knew he had worn a line in one of the front incisors, and Bob stood his ground in Steve's shadow. "See mine, Steve," he invited. "They're all perfect. I don't bite line. You have to use snipping pliers, nail clippers, or a sharp knife. Save your teeth," he enjoined them. Looking back and forth at each other, they promised to follow the mandate as set down by their master teacher. In the lesson, they forgot the tailing bonefish.

Still shimmering in the afternoon sunlight, the active school of feeding fish moved in its undulating and foraging rhythm. The three lads panted in laughter as they entered the water. They tried to conceal the amusement they felt from Bob's tirade on the "serious" issue just presented to them. Their stalking of prey began to separate them from the boat, but Bob had enjoyed having their undivided attention. He slipped into the water with his sneakers, trailing after them on their quests.

A second, smaller pod of fish materialized north of the boat, and the three separated onto individual tracks. Adam and Steve took the top and bottom of the larger school, while Kirk moved toward the smaller grouping. Bob hovered amid the two feeding groups. He never approached closer than thirty yards of any of the fishermen.

"Fish on!" bellowed Steve. Everyone froze and fixed his riveted attention on Steve. The hook-up was far enough below Adam's position that it did not startle the school. Steve's fish raced farther south away from the pod. Everyone heard the scream of line rushing from his reel. They detected the knifing of line in the water as it chased the bullet run of the bonefish. He would be busy for awhile, and Adam continued to lay his fly stealthily on the water near the north end of the school.

"Whoa! I got one," announced Kirk. He notified his comrades prematurely, for the limp line revealed the failed effort. His school moved, not in panic, but almost indifferent to him.

"Stay in touch with that group, Kirk." beckoned Bob. The elder guide began a slow stroll tracing Kirk and his movements to keep apace of his pod. Bob slid each footstep over the chalky bottom in a practiced gait that would prod skates and rays from his footfall.

Kirk looked back toward Bob and saw that Adam now had a fish in tow. It was a smaller one, for it was coming to his side already. Steve had yet to land his fish, and it now fought him some seventy-five yards from his companions. Every cast Kirk made seemed to push the school farther from him. Did they know he was there? Why were they not scattering in fright? Bob reached a whispering distance of Kirk.

"They aren't spooked, Kirk" assayed Bob. "Hold still a moment. Don't cast" he instructed.

Kirk held his ground reluctantly as the fish were moving from him, slowly on the prowl for bait. He waited. A glance at Bob told of his anxiety to get back into the hunt.

"Kirk, pick out a spot, a target, to lay the fly, somewhere away from the pod as far as you can haul," he advised.

Kirk opened his left palm upward as he secured the rod in his right hand. The tip pointed upward sixty degrees from his body. "Uh? Why do I want to do that?" was his doubting entreaty.

"Make a long cast with a double haul at one o'clock and just let it sit there," was Bob's unflinching answer. He watched the trusting youth lay the fly as directed. The school was twenty yards from the fly and heading west away from the pair. "Leave it sit, Kirk. Trust me," he added.

The school wandered about making random turns seeking crabs and shrimp. Coincidentally, it recoiled back on its trek until the group approached the pair of humans. To the bonefish, the men were no more than two-footed mangroves. Kirk wanted to recast to the school, and Bob caught him before he moved the line. "No! Wait another couple of seconds and then twitch the fly, just enough to stir up the bottom," he mandated. "That'll take up any slack, too."

Kirk did as instructed and with the quick pulse on the fly, the school swung in unison toward the motion. He was gaining confidence in this scheme of Bob's.

"They're almost on it. Twitch it again so they can find it," drilled the guide. Before he could add another piece of wisdom, Kirk's line was taut, and the reel was whirring to a melody that Kirk would never forget. "Fish on!" yelled Bob to the vast ocean and the two fellow mates south of his position. "Now that was fun!" celebrated Bob, pumping his right fist in repeated jabs into the air in front of him. Berger's Flat had produced another glorious day of bone fishing. At the ramp, Bob would be dutifully excused to open his shop and check for messages, mail, and Jan.

* * *

But as it were, he was just returning from his afternoon in the dark confines of Woody's gentlemen's club. The lads packed up gear, mopped up the deck, and hitched the Hewes to its trailer. Jan was still in her office when Bob sauntered in without giving any of the details of the day. She was in the process of closing for the day but informed him, "I'm running out on an errand, but I'll be right back."

"I have to wait for my ride anyway," was Bob's contribution to the departure.

"Okay, I'll meet you back here in your shop," drifted from the front door as she left him standing on the threshold of the "Keep You in Stitches" shop. "It's locked, Bob. Just pull the door shut!" she requested.

Business details were dispatched at Bonefish Bob's by the time the three young men entered the shop. The interior was graying due to the diminishing late afternoon light. Bob flipped on the light switches for the shop. The practice became a habit before closing each day. Good businessmen did not turn away last minute customers. Steve, Adam, and Kirk bounded into his midst with the exuberance of conditioned athletes after a hard fought victory. Kirk remembered with gratitude, "That was some great trick I learned out there, Bob! I remembered when you told Steve, 'Don't chase bonefish—let them come to you.' It worked. It really worked!" He expounded on his new-found tactic, and the others elaborated on the merits of Berger's Flat.

Bob, however, was overwhelmed with their energy. He felt somewhat relieved when a car ground to a stop in the lot. A minute later Jan swept into the shop. She was carrying two six packs of beer which she presented to the nearest male. The selection she handed to Adam was a mixture of various brews: light and dark, ales, porters, and pilsners.

"Thank you very much!" greeted Adam to the offering. His friends took the trophies from her, served her kisses on her cheek, and made sure she had one of the beers in hand.

"Thanks, Jan! That was quite a nice errand you ran!" voiced Bob, bursting with pride at her thoughtfulness. She remained long enough to politely finish her obligatory brew.

"You, Fellows, behave yourselves and drive carefully," was her parental parting advice.

An hour later, dinner plans were formulated, and Bob stood and stretched his legs. It was apparently a signal to the boys who immediately rose and bunched together. The threesome exchanged embraces, slaps and pats on the back. Bob greeted these antics with silent acceptance, for he realized that he had not shared the fishing with them that day. Still there was something familiar about the happenings before him. Adam turned from the trio and faced Bonefish Bob. "We're not letting you out of this," he delivered. "You're the one that got us started on this 'hugging' thing." A rush of friends was upon him, full of laughter, warmth and the goodness of life.

Chapter Fourteen

"The Retreat to Montana"

*As told in part by Jan Wood
and by Robert E. Berger to
Arthur Berger and to Stephen F. Blanche*

The timetable for the end of the Florida season varied with family obligations, visitors, the weather, and the couple's moods. Usually, the drive into the Northwest occurred in late May. The Montana lads had already left for their scheduled trips on the Clarkfork, the Smith, Rock Creek, and the Blackfoot Rivers. Jan and Bob traveled as light as possible, having left clothing and supplies in Ennis. The lightweight clothing of Florida remained in Islamorada except for the wares that were needed for the drive. Jan would stay in Montana as long as she chose, eventually summering there; but Bob, at first, had his sights set on spending more of his summers in Islamorada with his business. York became a destination for short family visits. A one-way airline ticket could take Jan home to Florida, or she could head east with Bob in his truck for a visit to York. The ritual held no hard and fast rules and went smoothly every year.

In transit, they sometimes visited friends or stopped at Jimmy's at his Dania Beach marina, but the trip remained unscheduled and unrushed. It was Bob's intention to set up a hermitage in Ennis, and Jan understood his need to find isolation and meditation in the eastern slope of the Gravelly Mountains. The venture each season was all uphill from the sea level flats of Florida through the mile high passes of the Rockies. Ennis was a small town nestled just north of the lap of Idaho that extended eastward along Montana's southern border. Wyoming nudged into the lower side of the state. Irrigated circular swatches of green dotted the flatter area to the north and east along the Madison River. The harsher and more arid western side of the town was washed in browns and earth tones. The Madison diverged into many parts as it ran its course and it left the landscape grateful for its moisture.

The cabin was situated in the foothills and the dry ridges just north and west of the town of Ennis. Bob considered it an act of God the day he purchased the cabin. Its view was eastward into the rising sun just like his shop in Islamorada. The façade was dressed with half-logs brought up from Yellowstone National Park. They were milled in halves and set to fortify the exterior from the harsh winters. The terrain of the property was left to nature; there was no attempt to manicure its surface or maintain the shrubs and foliage that were native to the countryside. The lower floor of the residence was Spartan: a bathroom, living room, small functional kitchenette, and a small bedroom. The second floor remained an unfinished loft. Bob and Jan spent the first days of occupancy each season mending the wear and tear of the past year on their aging retreat. The original owners had slapped some plaster over the seams that ran the perimeter of each four-by-eight sheet of plywood that made up the interior walls. Jan did some plastering to coat the walls and give them a more solid appearance. Bob fretted over the exterior, especially the roof. He maintained the heating, electrical and plumbing systems so as to provide a problem-free summer for Jan. He made certain that very little of his mental relaxation and fishing time was forfeited. Jan visited downtown Ennis, read extensively as any English major might, and hiked when the spirit came upon her. They prized the time spent breathing the snow scented air, wading the cool running trout waters and witnessing the rustic beauty of their hide-away.

Bonefish Bob sought various locales for fishing—the Madison River, the Ruby, and several ponds nearby. The Upper Missouri ran both hard and soft over a myriad of terrain and bends. It tumbled over rounded, water-eroded stones with the torrent of the heavy snow run-off or cascaded quietly among gentler rivulets and flats.

As Bob's hip began to act up, he settled on the Madison for wading. In his later years, this river became his preferred haunt. The "Fifty Mile Riffle" drew a straight line of restful waters near Ennis. The steady five mile per hour flow from the monitored effluent of Hebgen Lake grew large rainbows, browns, some cutthroat, and an occasional "cut-bow". Bob tied caddis, salmon flies (big stonefly nymphs) and blue-winged olive imitations for his trips to these tranquil waters. This stretch of river generally drew many tourists and first-time fly fishermen, and Bonefish Bob tolerated them.

His excursions to the Upper Missouri, however, were solitary events. Over numerous visits he had discovered one stretch of the stream that gifted him with great inner peace and serenity. It bred abundant native trout and an infinite variety of fishing sites: deep pools that ran lethargically, shallow water impoundments formed by natural boulder dams, violently rushing cascades of snow fed water, low trickles of wash off a main trunk, narrow riffles, and flats whose broadness challenged the fly fisherman's best casts. Every year these became part of Bob's memory, for the fish were plentiful and people were non-existent.

After parking his truck off the shoulder of the gravel road or being dropped by Jan, Bob began his familiar trek into the Montana wilderness. The trail he wore over the many visits to these grounds was difficult and exerting. He carried a backpack, fishing gear, light-weight waders and wading boots. An hour and a half or two hours into the trail, depending on distractions like elk or bear, he would break, suit up and commence fishing. Bob savored the work and effort, relished it like a runner's high after a lengthy jog. For Bob, it became a ticket of sorts, permission to walk among the treasures of life and enjoy his skill as a fisherman. He had, in his mind, earned the time there.

On one particular morning, he brought a five-weight rod and some lighter tippet material. His intention was to work his way upstream fishing an assortment of nymphs, then emergent insects, and then work into some dry fly patterns. A perfect day would be to land a fish at each water level of the stream with insect flies which he tied himself. The unknown variable surfaced, "On which ones were they feeding?"

He entered the stream without rod or reel and busied himself turning over rocks and stirring up the stream bed. He identified stone fly larvae, caddis, and others aquatic stages of the local insects. The clues were there and now the test commenced.

He drifted smaller size stone flies in three and four feet of moving water. The flow was meandering rather than rushing, and he availed himself of a "dead-stick" presentation. A gentle roll cast and the immediate mending of line upstream allowed the nymph to take on the pace of the current as it sank to the bottom. "No takers," he mumbled to himself.

Success finally came after he tied another pattern, opting for a pheasant tail in a size which matched some of the larvae he picked up earlier. A flip to the adjacent bank, which contained an undercut, rewarded him with a torrid, flailing run from a brown trout that rolled into the current to take his nymph. The fish dashed downstream with tail driving vibrations that the rod absorbed, allowing Bonefish Bob to control its wild scurry. When the fish veered to rush upstream, it leaped in frequent low arcs with such speed that Bob was hard pressed to gather in the line and disperse the slack onto the water below him. At the other shore, the brown settled into the depths, shaking its head with violent thrashings. Bob now had the line taut enough to feel the fish bite the fly repeatedly in its attempt to swallow or dislodge it. The five-weight took over and subdued the feral trout, and Bob released it without touching it. The barbless shank slid easily from the mouth of the brown with a little assistance from Bob's forceps. "Nice little gift there," he directed into the Montana air.

Having succeeded with fish at the bottom thermal of water, he now directed his sights on trout feeding on the emerging insects. Insects leaving the water as adults in a hatch would be a catalyst for a feeding frenzy. The later morning air revealed only occasional insects breaking free of the water. The water temperature was low and the morning air had not yet warmed the Upper Missouri enough to trigger a sizable hatch. He traipsed upstream to a swifter ripple with water in the two to three foot depth.

After tying on an eastern caddis, emerging pattern, he sought out underwater boulders and logs as targets. The strike would be a matter of feel with the "emerger", for he placed each cast well above his target, mending the line so as to draw the fly over or around the underwater obstruction. Instead of picking the fish he sighted, Bob chose the likeliest holding spot. Several casts drifted passed many likely protected areas, but a lack of interest in his offering prompted him to change flies.

On his third cast with an Adams, he cast to his left to the ten o'clock position before he drifted the fly in a sweeping motion into the current cascading around a large rock. At the slightest touch, almost a bump from a wind zephyr, Bob raised the rod tip and set the resistance on the unseen prey. A silver flash! "Rainbow on!" he welcomed. Its green back blended with the surface water as the fish charged toward Bob. The fish sought cover in the spread of Bob's stance. Pole high and left hand drawing in line at a rapid rate, the fly fisherman took control of the darting Upper Missouri rainbow. From his feet, the rainbow crossed the stream. The fish increased its power by playing the current against Bob's line. He doled out line for fear of breaking the tippet or disengaging the hook. The extra drag from the increased amount of line, however, worked against the rainbow. It wearied faster than Bob anticipated. He released the eighteen inch fish with delight. "Didn't expect that!" he mused.

A pool of flat, smooth moving water presented Bob with a pristine dry fly arena. Top water flies in Montana evolved into foam imitations designed by the guides. Their motto was, "Foam or go home!" Bob smiled to the fresh air as he attached a grasshopper to his shock leader. The Florida "Slams" were on his mind as he challenged himself to complete his personal contest against the three temperature gradients of the Upper Missouri. It was easier than he thought it would be. Several browns engulfed his "hopper", but he continued to cast until a sizable fish took the fly. The "take" brought the huge speckled back of the fish out of the water with just a sputter of a splash. "Big fish," hummed

Bob as the weight of the monster pulled a wide bow into his five-weight. The huge fish forced Bob into a stream walk as he followed its runs, sometimes racing after the fleeing brown. The pool was fifty yards long and Bob worried that the fish might opt to run into the rapids at the lower end. He leaned heavily against its bullish drive, just enough to turn it from its objective. Sweat marked his forehead and his thighs burned, but he sensed the subtle changes in the dynamics of the fight. The speed, the jumps and the intervals of each effort ebbed. Bob knew that he only needed patience to land the fish once that point had been reached. In ten minutes, the six pound brown rolled slowly back into the pool, released and free of the fisherman's tether.

Noon forced a rest period on the bearded Mainer. He sat in the silence, cherishing the day, and ate the provisions he had trucked into the Upper Missouri watershed. Hydrated, rested and refreshed, Bob walked to his favorite hole upstream. Today, he intended to make just a few casts on this stretch of water. He would then work his way downstream from this point, using streamer patterns. Whether he caught fish here or not made no matter to him. The desire to "save" this location for another day mellowed his aggressiveness. He tied a deceiver onto the tippet, knowing full well that it was not the best choice. Rounded boulders kissed the western side of the stream. Bob always approached the pool from this side, and his afternoon shadow played on the surface as he faced the water. He used care to avoid dabbing the surface with his reflection. Fishing was difficult enough without signaling stream-side your presence to the quarry.

A wall rose from the water on the far bank. The swing of the current nuzzled the roots of trees and the grasses which overhung the eastern side. The elevation could be sensed at this part of his trek; and, as he plodded farther north to the top of the rapids, he was aware of the exertion. A cascade of water sang over the natural steps which descended behind him. He set up for his target downstream. A back cast swept flat and rearward avoiding branches which impinged on the edges of the pool. He then elevated its pitch to allow for the rise of the rapids behind him. The forward power stroke sent the line before him, and it curled upon itself and headed for the water. Stripping the line back in jerking tugs, he simulated a darting baitfish. The loose, retrieved line floated in the current and worked its way downstream toward the center of the pool. He saw a shadow flicker behind his deceiver—the fish checked it and peeled off toward the steep bank. "That was a good size fish!" stammered Bob. The temptation to stay and fish the spot hard began to work on him.

Knowing the terrain, the effort needed to return and the distance from his parked vehicle, Bonefish decided to hold firm to his plan. He made a mental note about the fish at the head of the pool and made two more casts. Each targeted cast provoked a curious fish from its habitat, but neither struck the deceiver. He stepped from the water, eased himself along the boulder strewn bank and headed south.

Bob started fishing Clouser minnows and woolly buggers after he clipped off the deceiver. Working homeward in the long descending stretch below the pool, trout were taken with each of the streamer patterns. He elected to leave the Clouser on for the remainder of the return.

The Upper Missouri elbows itself downward in riffles and rapids to the west after the pool. A sound brought him stationary at the first bend. He distinctly heard a motor. Was it a plane or an auto? Before he could clearly evaluate the noise amid his perfect wilderness, the hum was gone. *That's unusual!* He pondered. Bob toyed with an answer, *probably a plane.* During his momentary pause, he unconsciously swung his vision north in the direction of some disturbance near the pool. Out of habit, he focused on the water as it descended from the north. From his peripheral vision, he thought he picked up a movement in the wooded area of the pool on its eastern side. There was a glint, a sparkle, a blur moving westward. *A woman . . .* posed Bob, *I must be dehydrated and damn tired.*

Troubled by the event, Bob fished little more on the return. He made a few test casts at rising fish, but found himself unusually concerned about the possibility, the odd appearance of an intruder, perhaps a woman, in his wilderness. Annoyance surfaced in his mood as he remembered the boys on the bridge who had trespassed on his fight with the huge tarpon. He felt deprived of the pure personal experience, of the unknown in the unfolding of the event, and of the individual physical challenge. Bob disliked having to share them with strangers and sometimes, even friends. It was disconcerting to him. Throughout his whole life, he shared his time with others: family, friends, and strangers. He wanted to possess these solitary events as his, uniquely his.

On his return to the cabin, the topic of Jan's day was open for discussion, but his day was not. Jan knew the routine of his fishing excursions; and she learned that, if he wanted to share some event, he would. This trip merited silence as far as she knew or understood. A cookout eased him into the evening and brought him peace and familiar ground. Jan volunteered to handle the greens and Bob managed the protein. They stood on the attached porch finishing the dinner wine. That completed, they faced Ennis side by side with their arms folded over their waists. The chill of the darkening air rested scintillatingly on the skin. Bob turned and took Jan in his embrace, rubbing her back briskly to induce warmth. The soothing contact was comforting to both after a day spent apart.

Chapter Fifteen

"Planning Chaos"

*As told in part by Robert E. Berger to
Arthur Berger and Stephen F. Blanche*

Bonefish Bob, aka BFB and Robert E. Berger, earnestly promoted the unknown in his life. His pranks, engaging demeanor, challenging fishing soirees, patient hunting, the wealth of friends, his businesses and his stories bred the unexpected, the laughable, and the inspiring. On more familiar ground in this lifestyle, he wooed certainty. It promoted the contingency plans he formulated to permit chaos to evolve through these events. He studied fish, animal characteristics, equipment, weather conditions, people and likelihoods. A childish revelry churned freely within him. This facet made him a voracious consumer, storing up resources and preparing to take on life and all its complexity. In another phase he was like bamboo, transforming into an adolescent, growing and evolving rapidly in reaction to the newness of each adventure. His cribbage and chess permitted him to sample a third level, the less hurried, deeper maturity of his own aging process. His understanding of the "World According to Bonefish Bob" was as fluid and complex as the tidal flow from the York River or the tumbling, gravity-fed effluent of the Upper Missouri.

During the week following his last journey to his favorite spot on the Upper Missouri, Bonefish Bob more or less wandered about Ennis. He spent a day at the Madison Meadows Golf Course. Unsettled, he botched a few short putts that he attributed to a lack of concentration, but the day was quietly enjoyable anyway.

The local ponds where he sought easy, relaxed fly fishing afforded him a day to rest his sore hip and practice a few of his various casting techniques without the bother of mending line against a current. He had a difficult time keeping Devil out of the water and abdicated the pond to the dog's frolic. The fish settled deep with Devil in the water, but the practice was still valuable. He did not mind the smell of the damp dog returning in his truck to the cabin. Jan insisted that Devil and sometimes Bob dry off and clean up before she allowed them into the place.

Their voluntary partnership managed the shopping chores in town that week. Bob found a deeper contentment with Jan during the week, and he accompanied her to the grocery and post office. They had lunch at The Reel Decoy on West Main Street. With a cold beer in hand, Bob looked quite content in his vacation mode. When Jan finished placing her order, she posed, "What are your plans for this afternoon?"

"I'm going to let the day tell me," he responded. His delivery seemed a bit brief to Jan. A suspicion that he really wanted to give her more information lingered in the silence amid sips of her Pinot Grigio and his Steelhead ale. Bob surprised her when he added, "The Upper Missouri's off-limits until next week."

Jan did not know how to respond to this strange revelation. This was not the type of comment he usually made. "Why do you say that, Bob?" she asked.

"Well, you know my hip's sore, and that spot I like isn't private anymore," confessed Bob. The ale to his lips momentarily halted the oozing of details from him.

She tested the waters gently, "How do you mean 'private'?" she queried.

Bob squirmed on the wooden bench, seemingly uncomfortable with the question. He placed the blame on himself for letting the matter pop into the light of the Ennis day. It left him pursing his lips. "Ah . . . , I don't know if I imagined this or not," he struggled, "but coming back I could have sworn I heard a car. Then I saw a glimpse of a woman, I guess, up at the big pool."

Bob had enough trust and faith in Jan to air childish doubts with her. The weightiness of this seemingly small matter became measureable to Bob only when he left it go. The buoyancy in his psyche overcame him following his statement, and he exhaled with the rush of full breath. He slouched and toyed with the label on the Steelhead.

"You didn't want to run into anyone, did you?" she surmised. His disappointment was shared mutually, for Jan knew how relieved and refreshed he became when he gorged on solitude.

"Nope! And I was charged up planning the trip back. It just took the wind out of my sails." He felt better already, but Bob was not yet eager to face an epiphany of inner reflections and personal turmoil. The waitress arrived. Facing the delivery of ribs and a salad, that comment was as much as he was willing to risk at the moment. "Man, these look great!" he judged, greeting the waitress with a broad smile. "With this beard, Young Lady, I'm going to need a few more napkins, okay?" he laughed as did Jan and the waitress.

"Just give it a little time. It'll be fresh again." Jan busied herself moving the plates, glasses and flatware to accommodate the food. The waitress passed by depositing a bundle of paper napkins and her friendliest smile.

"I intend to enjoy these ribs and spend a little extra time around the cabin." The ribs were messy. He delineated his plans amid the mechanics of the meal. His solution to the privacy matter seemed vague although Bob knew his objectives were exacting. He would return to the pool exactly one week later and at the exact same time. Bonefish Bob figured that would alter the time continuum, and the past would cease to be.

* * *

The truck sat in the driveway, ignorant of the taunting and teasing from Devil. The Lab cavorted about the vehicle like a child around a Christmas tree. Unsettled, it paced and yapped in expectation of Bob's arrival. As if rebellion were part of Devil's cognition, the dog nosed over to the passenger side rear tire, picked up the scent it wanted and urinated on the wheel. The cabin door creaked open.

"Get away from that truck, Devil!" ordered the hurried voice of Bob. He was charging down the path to the truck, energized with the future's plans and mysteries. "You aren't going today, My Friend," was his heart-felt apology to Devil. The dog amazed Bob as it retreated immediately to the porch with no apparent loss of joy. "Damn animal understands more than most people," he muttered with satisfaction.

The vehicle wheezed to a halt at the usual parking spot at his base camp for the journey to the fishing pool. Bob planned to rest his hip and hydrate at a site he had used frequently. That was his pre-assault camp. The final ascent would be glorious and like a thoroughbred race horse, he chomped at the bit.

The first stage of his trek had little to do with fishing. He transported his gear and opted to suit up when he reached the midway point. Bob tied one of his foam damsel flies to his tippet, determined to seek out only larger browns. With his other gear and food still stowed in his backpack, he fished sporadically from the shoreline. His selections of targets in the current flow were specific to this plan. He avoided smaller rifts and shallower water. Bob identified and attacked undercuts, boulders and deep pockets off heavy running current. Today, however, he lacked the patience to stay with each selected location. Even when his polarized lenses pinpointed lurking browns nesting in ambush, his limbs itched to move up-river. Driven by compulsory emotions, he could endure only two or three casts. The temptation to ascend the stream's elevation was overpowering.

At mid point, he ate sparingly, drank bottled water and unpacked his gear. He sat on a mossy fallen aspen low to the earth. A sense of the inner workings of his body induced him to straighten his legs before him and enjoy the tingling stretch of calf and quad muscles. The hip felt good. His respiration was accelerated, and he sensed the earthiness of the air that hung at ground level. It was his breathing rate that he sought to control with a series of slow, long inhaling breaths through his nostrils. He pushed the emptying exhales from his mouth in a gush of smooth, steady wind. This mental discipline trained him to take this time to prepare his body for what might lay ahead.

On foot once again and in his waders, Bob picked a small stretch of still, deeper water to test the effectiveness of the pattern. As he scanned the Upper Missouri waters trying to find the most advantageous target, a hatch began to boil from the water. Ever-widening poke marks on the surface announced the emergence of the dry-winged adult insects from the water-bound larvae. Silent explosions in watery indentations erupted into a swirling whirlwind that was choreographed by the summer air. Increasing into a tan, black, and gray cloud, the winged hatch rose as if smoke billowed from the waters. Chasing after the larvae in their attempt to fly, trout were rising, sucking the air-water mixture at the surface, engulfing the fleeing insects. These were large Montana stone flies.

Paralyzed by the dance and warfare, Bonefish Bob envisioned foxholes filled with exiting warriors, chased by a known, but unseen, enemy. Admiration for the complexity of nature with its beauty and violence, its mystery and practicality, and its beckoning and revulsion fixed him statuesque. Bob was bewitched like the bronze fly fisherman displayed on Ennis's Main Street. Minutes passed and, as the hatch began to dissipate, Bob swung into action. "What am I thinking? Don't want to miss this chance," he stammered into the wonder-filled afternoon.

He secured a newly chosen fly which matched the hatch of insects to his tippet. He fished the diminishing hatch, but it still boiled with commotion. To Bob it was a gift, a turn of fate. His fly was not lost amid the thousands of real insects on the water. A take pulled a diminutive brownie from the pool. "How the hell can such a little guy like you hit a fly this size!" he disciplined the five inch fingerling. A warble rose in his throat, almost a giggle, but he coughed to rid himself of it.

The pool held many smaller fish. Bob was tiring of their presence and after awhile, he found them to be a nuisance. Determined to move on, he made one last attempt to garner a larger specimen that he spotted hovering near a sunken bush. The fly fluttered onto the surface seven feet up stream of the feeding trout. Its course, guided by Bob's mending, inched closer to the inquisitive, foraging fish. Before Bob's fly arrived, the fish darted from the bush, appeared to take an insect at mid level, and rolled back to its haunt. Surprised to see another meal in its environs, it rose reflexively and struck the fly. Constrained by the small area of water which encased the trout's haven, the fish first attacked the rod and line with a single, vertical leap. The impoundment of the pool corralled the brown. The fish leaped again, eye-level to Bonefish Bob as he stood in the tail water of the hole. After each subsequent jump, the big brown anchored itself on the bottom, adding weight to itself by deep thrusts of its head. Bob held tension on his prey and increased the rod's power by raising the tip into the blue summer sky. Jump and settle became a pattern that lasted minutes until the fish plied another tactic. Quick left and right sprints of very short distances tested Bob's ability to control the trout. This method, however, began to fatigue the fish. Bob read this ploy as a last ditch effort on the part of the brown to find its freedom. Soon the five pound, two-foot-long German brown came alongside Bob's waders.

"Glad to have made your acquaintance." Bob introduced himself formally to the fish. Unhooked, the brown sank heavily to the bottom at Bob's left wading boot. "You're a little more spent than I thought," he addressed the struggling trout. Bonefish Bob was able to reach down and secure the exhausted fish by its mouth and then hold it by its tail. He cradled its underbelly in his left hand. The Thomas and Thomas rod with its Islander IR3 reel was tucked into the crook of his armpit. Slowly but gently, he pushed the fish forward repeatedly. At first, it remained limp in his hands, but soon he sensed the tail twitch and the head move. After a few more assists from Bob, he released it into the pool. Bob Berger was tired, relaxed, and elated.

The fifteen minutes he spent at the small pool transformed him, for the anxiety he sensed earlier evaporated in this contest of insect versus trout versus man.

The right hand bend upstream on the Upper Missouri came into view. Bob recognized the bottom of the long descent from his pool. Gathering himself just short of the curve, he planned to fish from the west side beginning at the lower end of the pool. He wanted to work dry flies northward toward the stepped cataract that marked the pool's head. The higher bank on the east side would be visually notched to judge his casts and mark his progress to the northern cascade. Casts would follow in sequence from near side to middle to far side. He liked his decision.

Bob forded the current to the westerly side of the turn. He positioned himself on the shadowed bank. As he ascended the elevation, he toed the shallows of the stream and, at times, trod the grassy edge. A pause to check his hip and his aerobic condition afforded him a glance upward to the pool, sixty yards from his position.

"Wha . . . uh? No, no!" fell from his throat. Ahead of Bob on the eastern bank was a man facing across the stream to the west. Bonefish Bob Berger turned homeward, head bowed and dejected. Something snagged him as he veered southward. Anger, curiosity, disappointment and adventure mixed into a batter of emotions unfamiliar to him.

"No, no!" was his denial, "I'm staying!" He countered the impulse to retreat with an aggressive stance. The situation would not deter him from his plans. Bob angrily took charge of the feelings, the thoughts and every muscle that wished him away.

Since the other fisherman had taken the pool before Bob, his only recourse was to ease his way northward and bypass the gentleman and the pool. He would circle the water from land and find a suitable area to fish beyond this position.

Twenty yards upstream and Bob became cemented to the earth when he refocused on the man. Behind some shrubs, Bob could see that this man was not fishing. He appeared to be seated and his general posture was a bowed head. The man was reading. Bob's thoughts raced over many courses as he waited for some idea or action to move him forward or in retreat.

Without realizing it, he had already taken several leaden steps forward. Twenty yards from the intruder and the pool, he hesitated in a rushing flat of water that dashed over tiny pebbles and gravel. His approach was steady but stealthy. The man had no sense that anyone had arrived. Again espying the seated stranger, breath abandoned Bob with his newest discovery. The man read from a wheelchair.

Bob now felt like the thief, stealing the serenity from this stranger in this man's retreat, his personal Shangri-La. Fearful that he might startle the gentleman, Bob ceased to cast or wend his way upstream. *Now, what?* he mused to himself. This was his day to fish, but something ridiculously unusual had altered that. This was his day to answer some nagging questions, but now he had even more. This was his day to bring normalcy back into *his* Upper Missouri, but now he found himself attached like a trout to a fly that it had never seen before. A deep, decision-making inhale, a sure step northward and his left hand waving the air, Bob signaled the man, "Hello, hello there!" Bob Berger had embraced the moment.

Chapter Sixteen

"Catch and Release"

As told in part to Arthur Berger and to
Stephen F. Blanche by Robert E. Berger

The stranger looked up from his novel and pivoted his head in the direction of Bonefish Bob. Only the upper torso of Bob was visible to the man, but he threw an amicable right handed wave at the ascending angler. He leaned back in the chair, resting from his forward reading posture. He awaited the arrival of the visitor.

The terrain drew much attention from Bob as he approached his quarry. The bottom was slippery and stones threw him off his balance. He did not wish to appear awkward to this man and, slowing his pace, he picked his pathway with more care than normal. Glimpses of the gentleman mixed with quick checks of the footing. Bob had little inkling of what the man looked like until he completely forded the stream and climbed the flat bank on the eastern side. Standing firmly on both feet facing the person in the chair, Bob drew in a few gulps of Montana air in the same manner that he would polish off a cup of lukewarm tea when he was in a hurry.

The stranger spoke first, catching Bob's pause to issue his first thoughts. "You need to get your breath after a climb like that," he initiated. Reading glasses hung on the bridge of his nose under a gray slouch hat embroidered on the front with a blue upper case "P".

"Yeah, it's taken me a few hours to get up here," responded Bob who had closed the distance gap with six sure steps. Bob examined the wheelchair and found the chrome and black leather out of place in the wilderness at the Upper Missouri.

"How's the fishing?" requested the man with an air lacking any seriousness, usual in trivial exchanges between new acquaintances. He wore a gray, red, and black plaid light-weight, long sleeved shirt and tan Dockers.

"Not too shabby!" boasted Bob who was pleased to be on familiar ground. "These new foam flies are killers!" The report produced no show of interest from this new comrade. Bob awkwardly attempted to keep his focus on the man's face. A complexion marred by wear and tear revealed an out-of-doors existence. His dark brown eyes were honest, filled with the earth and sun.

"I never took much to fishing, but I surely do enjoy the places you guys find," he volunteered in a reasoned, matter-of-fact delivery. As he turned over the novel, *Iracema's Footprint*, onto his lap to save his current page, Bob was privy to his condition as a double amputee. The folded material of his trousers was tucked neatly under the legs.

"This is, I guess, my absolute favorite spot to fish in fresh water," emphasized Bob as he laid his rod securely along the trunk of a mature tree. Setting up a comfort zone of sorts, he removed the backpack and pushed his polarized glasses onto his head.

"I come up here once a week religiously," offered Bob's new acquaintance. He twisted a quarter turn to face Bob more directly. The man was outfitted well for the climate and the insects.

"Yeah! How the hell did you get here?" imposed Bob before adding, "It usually takes me an hour and a half to climb the river bed to this point."

A wry smile formed on the gentleman's mouth. "There's an old logging road that comes to about forty yards of this spot. My daughter Claudia drives me up and wheels me in." His right hand gestured at his chair simultaneously with the word, "wheels". Bob figured the guy had a good sense of humor down inside somewhere.

Hearing the last comment from the reading man, Bob felt a hum, a tick, something working within his person. "I don't know why, but . . ." he searched for the phrasing, "your voice sounds familiar to me." Bob stood now just a handshake away from the fellow who was flipping his head from side to side. He had no such feeling about Bob. "Where ya from, anyway?" continued Bob.

Turning the back of his head to Bob, he indicated the back of his cap. "Indiana," was the single word response. Then his right hand index finger moved and pointed to the word, "Pacers," stitched in blue letters across the arched opening at the sizing gap of the hat.

"Oh! A basketball fan," surmised Bob. "Well, I've been to Indiana once." After a two count pause, Bob asked, "Are you visiting here for the summer?"

"No, I live here year round. My son-in-law's family is from here. Grandkids, you know. The wife wanted to be near them." The conversation became easier. Time dismantled the fences that both men abruptly assembled during the first spoken words. Sometimes, Bob found it easier to exchange the whiff and puff of his life with a stranger more readily than with a close acquaintance. The wheel-chaired man also possessed this trait.

Bob expounded on his exploits in Florida, Jan, and the cabin in the foothills of the Gravelly Mountains. The stranger revealed the daughter's success, her children, and the little place that they kept in downtown Ennis.

The talking quickly used up the surface incidentals of their present lives, and pauses lengthened between the answers and the questions. Bob turned to another issue, but he did so without a sense of probing or curiosity. "How'd you get injured?" dropped from his lips, smoothly without a glint of intrusiveness.

The Midwesterner peered into the blue eyes of Bob with a mechanical glance, hardened by countless similar questions. "Korea," was his brief fact.

"I was in Korea, too" was Bob's abrupt complement to the man's revelation. A respite ensued and the men absorbed the serenity around them. Breezes wafted their loose garments and refreshed their faces with a cooling touch. The steady comfort of gurgling water seeped into the rush of wind in bushes and the songs of birds flitting about the water's edge. Bob's confession produced a sense of mutual respect. Bob, however, bristled that his comment had slipped from him too easily.

As Bob stood facing the pool beside the wheelchair-bound veteran, the moments of casual reflection were internalized by each man. Neither one focused on the wants, needs or fears of the other. This meeting, which began by simple accident, now evolved into a challenge where risks were being calculated. Bob figured that whatever transpired at this pool on the Upper Missouri was taking root and could simply stay here. He found himself saying, "It was pretty rough over there." The delivery was dry, monotone and appropriate.

The ex-serviceman by his side looked up and studied the right side of his new Montana companion. Bob's beard rose and fell with gentle breaths. His arms were folded across his girth, and he rocked rhythmically from toes to heels. The Midwest-erner approved of him but momentarily found amusement in the gear that Bob wore. "You always get decked out to the hilt like this? I mean when you fish," he rattled off with light sarcasm. At the same time, he patted the right wader-clad leg of Bob with the back of his left hand.

"Oh, sure when the water's cold, but you have to be careful," Bob missed the jibe, "if there are a lot of brambles and thickets to come through." Bob took the remark as if made by a green client on a guided trip.

Tenuity was present in the subsequent silence as if some-thing was eager to be said, but it had anchored somewhere on the bottom. The Midwesterner shut his book which pulled Bob from his own musings.

"I spent a lot of time at the front, too, and saw some heavy fighting," the man admitted calmly. There seemed to be no battle raging within him. The truth came from him as data, unchange-able and accepted. This alleviated Bob's concerns that he might have transgressed on the privacy of the Midwesterner.

In his own defense, Bob contributed, "I don't talk about it much."

"I suppose I'm luckier that way because talking about the 'it' was part of my rehab," continued the veteran.

"So, how did you get wounded?" ventured Bob with a degree of comfort that emerged from their common ground.

The answer flowed easily. "Well, my buddies and I were hunkered down on the top of a little hill. The North Korean's brought in small artillery and mortars. I remember the cold, the dampness, trying to dig in on that open position. They were lobbing everything at us."

Bob twitched at the mention of the mortars; his attention drifted briefly beyond the details of the story. His companion continued speaking but Bob's inward drama left him deaf. Not until he picked up the word, "carried," did Bob's focus return to the man seated beside him. "Uh? Say that again," directed Bob of his storyteller.

"After the mortar detonated near me, my buddy carried me quite a-ways to a jeep he found. That fellow got me off the hill to a MASH unit." He seemed prepared to continue the story from that point, but Bob intervened abruptly.

Bob put out both hands, begging the man to stop his narrative. "I don't want . . . no, you can't go any farther with this," emotions of dread and fear rose in the raspy, throaty words.

"Okay," the man hesitated and then added, ". . . being a farmer, I know when the seed's in the wrong ground."

The phrasing, the lingering feeling, and the sound of the Midwesterner's voice put Bob Berger in such a chaotic vortex that he struggled to balance impossibility with hope and foolishness against a miracle. This was the unknown, the blow that was never expected. "Your voice. . . . My God, that comment . . . !" prayed Bob just before his spontaneous leap for clarity. "Someone else used to say *that* to me. You can't be Stony! You aren't Stony Van Hook, are you?" The effort and courage to ask the question stunned him and apparently the gentleman in the wheelchair as well. Bob stood before the man with his mouth pressed tightly shut. He had given voice to one of the Furies, and she could never return to her inner vault.

The veteran in the wheelchair sat with mouth agape, speechless. Bob was sure the man thought he was a lunatic. Men can converse for many minutes sharing their doings, but never exchange their names. The serviceman coughed. "I am. But how do you . . . ," he forced the few words from himself; faltering, he struggled with others which he had to leave unspoken.

Bob leapt into the sentence, the silence and the void. "My God! Oh, my God! I'm Bob Berger. I'm your buddy! I pulled you from that foxhole!"

"Great heavens! No way! How? Bob, it's really you?"

"Holy Lord! This is impossible!" beamed Bob, dropping to his knees beside Stony. It seemed as though Bob did not possess enough arms to express his joy with the happiest, most tear-filled embrace of his life. His arms patted, caressed, nudged and enveloped Stony. "You're alive! You made it, Stony!" sobbed Bob.

"Bob, thank you! Thank you!" repeated Van Hook into the body of Bob's fishing vest. "I never thought I'd get the chance to thank you."

"And I've kept you right here." Bob thumped his chest with a forceful drum of his right index finger. "I figured you died. No one ever let us know." The passing seconds and minutes allowed the photo-negative to develop into clarity and focus. Each man sized up and appraised the other: first a gentle push away, the close examination, and the drawing in for another embrace. "Stony, this is just too good to be true," weighed Bob.

"What are the odds? How did we get thrown together fifty years later?" Stony's question was rhetorical and accepted as unanswerable.

"I almost decided never to come back here when I heard the car last week. And I thought I was going nuts because I believed I saw a woman up here, too." Bob patted Van Hook's shoulder, shook his hand, and hugged him repeatedly. "I have this itch. I have to conquer things on my own, earn some solitary . . . privacy, you know," he explained.

"I am so glad you took the chance," said Stony, rubbing Bob on the back.

Bob knelt next to his friend along the bank and then sat with his feet dangling childlike over the edge. The old friends traveled great distances together in the discourse that ebbed and flowed. Van Hook liked Bob's new identity as Bonefish

Bob. Stony had some pictures of the grandchildren, and Bob proudly raveled off a litany of his brood. Appointments were set to have lunch together before Bob returned to the Keys. They would meet as many times as they could, but Bob opted for a less familiar spot on the southeast side of Ennis. They crammed as much reliving as possible into the happenstance before the rumble of Claudia's car was heard. The noise sputtered to silence, and the daughter approached with an unhurried gait from the logging road.

Van Hook's daughter was an energetic, caring woman. She held the men together in her presence for twenty minutes, trying to fathom the impossibility of their encounter. Only when assured that the men had definite plans to meet again did she willingly assist her father into the vehicle. They offered Bob a ride to his truck, but he graciously refused any transportation. He wished to digest the events of the day and come to terms with what Providence had given him as a gift. He slouched down to the passenger seat and faced his Army buddy in the auto. Enwrapping his brawn about Stony, Bob drew him tightly like a guide pulling on a synch knot. The daughter was filled with compassion and joy for her father. Claudia guided the wheeled apparatus from the car door and waited to fold it before storing it in the trunk. She stood on the opposite side of Bob. Spontaneously, the woman joined in their partnership and found herself kneeling with the two men in a long, silent farewell embrace.

He did not fish any more that day. With the arrival of Stony Van Hook, his solitary fishing plans exploded like confetti. As far as Bob Berger was concerned, this was the greatest fishing trophy that he had ever received. Arriving at the truck, Bob settled his emotions and took a long period of time packing his gear for his return. Lapping about in his mind to the rhythm of the tides in the sea was a notion, one private, and, for some reason, Bob felt, dangerous. By the time he reached the cabin, the events of the day were his and only his. His excitement contained and now controlled, he could face Jan without any revelations at all. If this miracle echoed into the light of day, all the long buried, dark days of Korea, the other Furies, would need to follow suit. His private fishing time had netted this reunion for him, and it would be guarded and honored in silent memorial.

The lunch happened. The little diner in Ennis sheltered their first appointed meeting. "Do you remember Timmy Holcolm that time at the driving range?" Stony reminisced. As Van Hook's wheelchair slipped back and forth under the table top, Stony moved to clamp the brake on the wheel. Bob watched the effort and dreamed that Stony was whole again.

"Sure. Yes!" spouted Bob with the full memory alive in his recollection.

"He was a classy lefty . . . until you put a golf club in his hand," detailed Stony as Bob pressed forward in the excitement of the old story. He took notice of how familiar Stony seemed. Despite his aging eyes, his forehead, mouth, and nose still possessed the vitality of a youth.

"That swing he took . . . spilled himself right off the driving range mat onto his backside. That's one of the funniest things I've ever seen," evaluated Bob, rolling backward in his seat with the laughter of an honest Santa Claus.

"Then . . . ," roared Stony, "the ball drops from the sky and smacks him right in the crotch!" Van Hook spouted the punch line like an erupting geyser. He checked the lunchroom to see if he had laughed his way out of bounds, but they were alone with their past.

A subsiding of the frivolity spiced the tales, and they gradually spoke of more mundane occurrences in the service. Bob felt the need to justify his private decision with his resurrected friend. "Stony, I haven't told anyone that I ran into you," he confessed.

"Why?" began Van Hook, and then in immediate reconsideration, "My family knows, and they're thrilled about it. But that's my slant on this. I don't know where you are with it."

"Look Stony, I don't talk to anyone about the war. My ex-wife, my kids, and Jan know nothing about it or about the guys back then. I've never breeched the issue because I don't want to ever go there again." Bob found the dialogue with Stony to be a neutral shade of emotion. Here his passive, almost indifferent, references to the war were less agonizing as he feared they would be if they sprang up within his family. When the temptation to reveal them came upon him, it sickened him, drove him onto the edge of depression. He medicated the ache with pranks, stories, activities and even his bourbon.

"I understand," was Van Hook's simple acceptance.

"If I give you up, I'll have to dredge it all up," whispered Bob across the table, now littered with the ort of the meal. "This whole thing . . . it has to be just mine."

"Hey! We had two separate lives until last week. We should be able to do what we want with this new connection that we have. You want to treat me like a Christmas present, you go right ahead." Van Hook did not feel like tampering with the Magi. He was content to have renewed his life with the man who had saved it so many years ago.

So they set up trips and future get-togethers. For Stony Van Hook, the journey enriched his family and local friends in Montana and Indiana. For Bob Berger, the visits confirmed the answer to his one, great looming question, *Yes, Stony Van Hook had lived.* Now Bob wondered if the lesser questions of his daily life held enough fuel to drive his love of life and its excitement.

Bonefish Bob had only two lapses in his privacy manifesto. One winter day he shared this Montana event with a young guide, Stephen F. Blanche from Pennsylvania and his fiancée, Nicole Elliott. For reasons known only to Bob, only one other person saw this miracle through his sea-blue mental eyes. In York, while visiting Art, he had related pieces of the same emotional tale of his Korean experience. Art kept it to himself as Bob had requested. Perhaps this young man and his girlfriend encountered Bonefish Bob at a similar meditative crossroad.

In Islamorada at Bonefish Bob's shop on that day, the young couple dropped in just as Bob was about to lock up for lunch. Both clerks had the day off. It was a particularly dark, overcast afternoon. Bob Berger slipped from the discussion of the practical business of fishing into a more somber series of philosophic topics. This was a prelude to the revelation of the events in Montana. The quick steps of his puttering about the shop while clambering on the art and science of angling switched, like the weather, rapidly into a stooped, shuffling gait. This "forced march with full pack" led him to a seat near the register. He was carrying an unseen weight upon his shoulders and a torrent in his soul. His demeanor during the telling was tearful. He sobbed freely, wiping the moisture from his cheeks and eyes with the lightweight sleeve of his shirt. The events simply oozed from him. The mesmerized couple had stood respectful, silent and concerned. The tale was hypnotic. In the end, Bob seemed sated beyond the story's containment. The miracle had its next unveiling in Maine, when circumstances necessitated its release through a pressure valve that only Bob could open.

Jan knew the name Van Hook, for Bob Berger mentioned that he had tried to visit the family of a deceased soldier in Indiana, but that he never located them. Bob rarely mentioned Korea, and Jan knew that he had terrifying dreams of his duty there. Briefly, and only once, Bob painfully recounted to her the fact that one day he had carried a wounded fellow soldier a "great distance" as he put it. Bob Berger confessed that, at the time, he "figured he was carrying a dead man" during the attempt to save him.

The other lunches happened. They met clandestinely in Ennis, near Miami and in Terre Haute, Indiana. Bob selected eateries that he had never frequented in unfamiliar locales. The meals were tasteless and easily forgotten, but the GI buddies were invigorated with good times and the joy of new life. The names from boot camp continued to dance into their conversation with zest and vibrancy. Neither Bonefish nor Stony dabbled in the menace and terror that had awaited them in the Orient. Here was now, and Bob prized it like a luxurious vacation that he had won in some contest. Van Hook and he tried to fathom the kindness and the purpose of the treasure that they were given by their unseen benefactor. Neither of the men was church-religious, but Bob embraced the marvelous and wonderful soul of Stony Van Hook.

Chapter Seventeen

"Tasting the Harvest"

Pieces told in part by James Berger,
Dr. H. C. Palmer and Jan Wood

The mystery and challenge of golf waned for Bob. He held his steady handicap, gaining little or no progress as the years took their toll. He was ever the teacher, however. Dr. H. C. Palmer and he had scheduled a round of golf at Keys Gate Golf Course in Florida City, and the day tested the good doctor more than Bob. After a disappointing result from a shot out of heavy Bermuda grass, "HC", as Bob called him, sauntered back to his bag and thrust the offending club briskly into its slot.

"Whoa there!" interrupted Bob, "you go throwing your clubs like that, and this'll be the last time I play with you." Bob meant it. The score of his round on the links had less importance for Bob now. He was content to be there, rather than to compete.

"I only pushed the club down into the bag, Bob," rationalized the doctor. The motivation for Bob's little criticism escaped him. HC and Valerie lived year round in Kansas, and the couple had fortuitously befriended Jan and Bob on their trips to the Keys. He soon learned that Bob always choose the appropriate time and place to offer good, sound advice. Dr. Palmer figured that this was one of Bob's "appropriate moments." There arose in Dr. H. C. Palmer a personal vow, an oath of sorts, to never again vent his disappointment as he had. To his credit, he would maintain that promise and remember Bob's off-the-cuff reprimand.

"The tally doesn't matter so much as the manner you use to get there," reflected Bob as a second thought. "You have to take the surprises in stride, HC."

"Never too late to learn, I guess," muttered the doctor mostly to himself. He preferred that Bob not hear that he had taken the suggestion to heart. HC received pardon from Bob for his offence when the good doctor bought the beers at the end of the round.

Other golfers who spent time with Bob at the various courses which he frequented attributed his mellowness to the act of maturing. Bob never gave it a thought—the style of his play simply evolved or just happened. Birdies, triple bogeys, great bunker shots, and poorly played putts had equal value. The time spent on the course with friends had worth, but the game sowed fewer and fewer rewards and even less disappointments.

The expectation and the unknown in his fishing trips evaporated into the sultry days of ongoing summers. He fought the fish that took his lures and flies; some escaped and others were landed. Great and small was the bounty, but the excitement of each foray dulled and faded like autumn days. The lust for the contest dulled like the honed edge on his favorite pocket knife. The sharpening stone could not be found to whet his appetite. An erasure moved silently throughout the bays, coves, streams, and rivulets and eroded their purpose and meaning. Either Bob ceased to search for the driving force to stimulate, tempt, and taunt his curiosity, or he just could not find it.

Jan and Bob harvested many fish for meals: snapper, sea trout, yellowtail, and groupers. Bait fishing with spin cast reels provided them with fresh fish for evening meals. The Atlantic Ocean side of Islamorada gave its harvest to those fishermen who worked the conditions and the habitats for these denizens. Bob would anchor with a chum line of oil oozing from the frozen net bag which held mackerel and assorted offal from the processing plant.

"Jan, keep both lines down near the bottom," encouraged Bob with a teacher's license. A shrimp was cut in halves and threaded through the carapace, leaving the barb unexposed.

"Do I have enough weight, Bob?" she queried with the seriousness of a pitcher taking a signal from the catcher. The days were calm and the seas manageable when they saw fit to bottom fish. Pinfish and runners lured by the melting sludge worked their way up the oily slick which trailed from the submerged net.

"We'll know in a minute or two," encouraged Bob, watching the rod tips for signs of a strike. "The scavengers have found the chum so you might let some extra line out on one of your poles." With that done, they now had four different depths and distances to work the bottom and the strata of water just above the reef where he settled the skiff.

A dribbling series of rapid pulses rang one of Jan's rods. "There's one, Bob," she announced as she began to pump the pole and reel the unseen fish to the boat. "I wonder what I've got."

"It's swimming like a little spot, back and forth," he guessed. The end of the brief battle brought a small red snapper on board.

"You're wrong, but you did get the size right," she teased. She laid the fish on the measuring tape affixed to the gunwale. "It's got to go back," sighed Jan with a hint of defeat.

"We'll get some more. Don't you fret, Jan. Dinner will be on this boat by the time we up-anchor." His premonition proved accurate, for he soon hooked a good sized grouper. The fish raced downward, struggling to embed itself in the coral of the reef. Bob understood its tactics and kept constant force on the burrowing grouper. On board, he deposited it into the live well.

Jan was excited to watch the stealth by which her long-time companion harvested the fish. "I'm going to get my chance right now," she cheered as her deepest baited rod shot down in the direction of the same reef. The dark island of vegetation and coral provided camouflage for the prey. She did not espy the fish in the fifteen feet of water beneath them. Surrounded by tan and milky sand, the struggling fish hovered above the reef and remained virtually invisible to Jan. The drag clicked, protecting the line from breaking, and Bob eased next to her.

"Let me tighten that drag down a bit, Jan." His request was approved, and she held firm to the weight of the fish as Bob manipulated the gear without the slightest interference to her performance. "Now, you'll be able to keep him off the bottom and get him boated sooner." His manner was businesslike, almost passionless.

"I can't see it, Bob. Can you tell what it is?" she begged as he busied himself with his own equipment. There was no audible answer, and Jan remained fixed and concentrated on the task at hand. "Oh! I see it! I see it!" Her voice echoed with the thrilling news.

While she fought the fish, Bob reeled in his lines and secured them in storage. He nudged along side of her with a large, wide-mouthed landing net. "That will be dinner," he announced. "With my grouper and this fish here, we'll have plenty of leftovers," he tabulated.

"I have to land it first, Bob," she tested. A glint of red sparked through the blue of the sea as the fish came off the bottom. "It's red . . . a big red snapper," she detailed to her boat mate. Ten more yards of line and the snapper was in the confines of Bob's net. He placed it flat on his yardstick. "Wow! That's what . . . a keeper!" she bubbled.

"Probably goes four or five pounds, Jan. That's a nice fish, Partner," he complimented. It was deposited into the well, and Bob began to break down her rods. The pieces of remaining bait on her hooks were tossed overboard.

"Aren't we going to stay and catch a few more?" wondered Jan with the same pang of remorse felt by a youngster taken from an amusement ride as the roller coaster comes to a halt.

"Nah! No need for any more," he decided. The practical purpose of the trip that started with the promise of dinner now abruptly ended with the filling of the larder. Bob did not sense Jan's bewilderment as he dutifully secured the gear and other articles for the trip back to the ramp at Bonefish Bob's.

* * *

His guide fishing, his shop, and his cribbage took on the same aura. On Christmas of 2005, Bob surprised Jan by deciding to spend the day with his son, Jim. The oldest of the brood lived just out of Fort Lauderdale. Jan and Bob had the habit of staying home during the holidays, and this was a bit unusual in Jan's thinking. Bob telephoned Jim, and the son's family was elated by the upcoming visit. Bob did not want to overstay the welcome or disrupt the festivities so he invited Jan and himself only for Christmas day. Of all the Berger children, Jim possessed the traveled wings of his father, venturing into the Coast Guard and then south out of Maine during his adult life. His habit of seeing Bonefish Bob monthly set up a communication system of sorts whereby the other siblings were in touch with their Dad vicariously. Robbie, Wendy and Judy accepted mother-keeping duty by staying near Lois in Maine.

The day went wonderfully. Bob brought his cribbage board, and Jim and his father spent most of the day engaged in their favorite pastime, playing cribbage. "The Board," as Jim referred to it, originated in antiquity in Maine. Bob had it for years before bringing it to the shop in Islamorada. No one was trustworthy or honorable enough to clean it or set pegs in it except the master, Bob, himself. The grandchildren frolicked about the home during the ongoing games. Jan and Jim's wife enjoyed the grandchildren, the kitchen, and the company of their men. As darkness overtook the celebration, Bob and Jan made ready to return to Islamorada.

"It was great that you and Jan could make it up for Christmas, Dad," cajoled Jim with pride and satisfaction that his home had been the recipient of a Bob Berger visit.

"It was overdue, Jim." Bonefish was polite and endearing with everyone, but especially his own children. The childhood cookouts and fishing trips bound them together with trust, love and an appreciation of the hard work that it takes to become a family. The length of the father-son embrace was so protracted that it found Jan and Jim's wife standing by shyly as silent spectators. Bob unwrapped himself from Jim's clutches, turned to the rest of the family and softly spoke, "You kids take care and be good for Mom and Dad. Jim, those kids are keepers. No throwing them back," he forced a chuckle into the room. He turned, ushering Jan from the home ahead of him. Almost free of the door's swing, he was halted by Jim's voice.

"Hey! Dad, you left the cribbage board on the dining room table. Wait a minute! I'll get it," rushed the words as Jim attempted to keep his father at bay. He had retreated only a few paces into the room when Bob spoke.

Holding the screen door back from its path with his left hand, Bob called after Jim. "Son, don't worry about it. Why don't you keep that cribbage board here for a change?" Jan looked wide-eyed, and her vision passed Bob and focused on the face of Jim. He wheeled about, caught off guard by the enormity of the gift. "Maybe it'll bring me up here more often," he suggested.

"Dad, this is 'The Board'," he uttered with reverence, "Are you sure you trust me with it? I mean it's been with you fifty years or so, hasn't it?" appraised Jim in a futile attempt to fathom the motive for the gift.

"It's Christmas, and that's Santa's present to you," wished father to son. Jim dashed to the front door in a last ditch effort for a second embrace. The encounter was rewarded by a hearty laugh which rose from a deep recess in the barrel chest of Bone-fish Bob.

Chapter Eighteen

"The Healing"

As told in part by Public Record,
Robert Berger II, and James Berger

On May 18, 2006, Jan was away. Bonefish Bob had nothing to do and wanted nothing to do. He picked up a favorite pen and a sheet of writing paper. The overcast sunrise left the trailer dark into the late morning. The lamps did little to move the shadows from the living room. A steady blow of westerly wind grated against the palms outside and sent sounds of rasping and rubbing into the room. The paper went unmarked from his hand and rested beneath the weight of the pen on the coffee table. Bob stretched from his Lazy Boy into an upright stance. He roamed the rooms of the home, touched his favorite rod and reel but postponed any possible fishing trip. The golf clubs nestled in the kitchen causeway. He tapped the head covers, entertaining a round, but decided against it. He shunned the challenge of the wind either at sea or on the links. The tea in his cup was lukewarm, and he left it for later.

Bonefish Bob traversed the spaces of his residence in no particular hurry. He dwelt on bric-a-brac and photos, some of which he had not perused in quite some time. He hummed a nonsense melody, part familiar lilt and part invention. The music was not his main concern. The grandchildren's pictures garnered a smile from him, and he considered some matters of their parents and their futures. *Great kids . . . great parents*, he mused proudly, considering the directions that their lives had taken. His role in their development came into focus for him like a Picasso cubist work. He was there for them, and he was not there for them.

They had their anchors down, and Jan and he had their foundations far from his children's harbors. Somehow it worked; they retained their individuality and independence much as Bob had journeyed to protect his. *They do have my genes*, he concluded philosophically.

A happiness and contentment enveloped Bob when he returned to his chair. "Jim got a kick out of my cribbage board," he uttered into the calm space before him. That gesture he made last Christmas uplifted him. Bob was amused that letting go of that memento had so gratified him. The hobbies that he had collected to himself had, like his old York tow truck, dragged his spirit into the unexpected, sometimes kicking and screaming. "All those glorious gifts!" he whispered in thanksgiving to the comforting air about him.

Bob concealed this ennui that had settled heavily upon him from his associates, the family, Jan and their friends. By his emoting of a feigned *status quo*, he had made a passable show. *They haven't seen the real Bonefish Bob in quite awhile*, he thought. *I haven't been exactly fair to Jan or the family with this charade.* As his behavior over the last months took on the semblance of an illness, Bob attempted a self-diagnosis. He sought a cure. The gift to Jim alleviated a great deal of the doubt and set him on a new course. A change from the pursuit of life's adventures prodded Bob to seek a true healing.

He picked up the paper and pen and jotted down a note to himself. The document went back onto the table top and rested beneath the stylus. With a sense of control that he had recently lost, Bonefish Bob accepted a courageous tact that presented itself to him as a pure quest, noble and independent in nature. Korea, the dangers of fishing on rough seas, and the precarious situations he survived while hunting loomed in fog-filled stories like a great novel that he once read.

An apparition of him teaching his young children the wiles of nature rose from his memory banks and satisfied him. The hours that he spontaneously gave to the children of others after his shop hours also pleased him. The youngsters mastered the basics of the fly cast with his lead, casting to a bucket in the parking lot. *I did well*, he appraised of those volunteered hours that he spent with the children.

Afoot again, Bob marched into his bedroom. He sought an old relic from his chest of drawers and picked it up. Enjoying the weight of the article in his hand, he carried it back to his seat. It took on his heat, losing the coolness that it had stolen from the bureau. Its temperature changed like the habits of his life, settling on lukewarm. Certain of the decision that had grown within him since the resurrection of Stony Van Hook, Bob looked confidently at the relic in his right hand, eased it upward and pulled the trigger.

Somewhere once, Robert E. Berger read a philosophical life-study. It had more church religion attached to it than he was accustomed, but its principles fit into the round pegs of his crib-bage board life. Many of the tenets, absorbed like a salve into his being, stayed with him.

"God has created me to do Him some definite service. He has committed some work to me which He has not committed to another.'

"I have my mission—I may never know it in this life, but I shall be told of it in the next. I am a link in a chain, a bond of connection between persons.'

"He has not created me for naught. I shall do good. I shall do his work. I shall be an angel of peace, a preacher of truth in my own place, while not intending it, if I do but keep His commandments. Therefore, I will trust Him. Whatever, wherever I am. I can never be thrown away. If I am in sickness, my sickness may serve Him; in perplexity, my perplexity may serve Him; if I am in sorrow, my sorrow may serve Him.'

"He does nothing in vain. He knows what He is about. He may take away my friends; He may throw me among strangers. He may make me feel desolate, make my spirits sink, hide my future from me. Still, He knows what He is about." It was The Prayer of Cardinal John Henry Newman, born in 1801.

The Islamorada Coroner's Office completed its primary investigation, and the conclusion centered on Bob's one sen-